VISITING THE SOMME AND YPRES

BATTLEFIELDS MADE EASY

GARETH HUGHES

First published in Great Britain in 2014
and reprinted in 2015 by
PEN & SWORD MILITARY
An imprint of
Pen & Sword Books Ltd
47 Church Street
Barnsley, South Yorkshire
S70 2AS

ISBN 978 1 47382 139 2

A CIP catalogue record for this book is
available from the British Library

Printed and bound in England
By CPI Group (UK) Ltd, Croydon, CR0 4YY

Pen & Sword Books Ltd incorporates the Imprints of Aviation, Atlas,
Family History, Fiction, Maritime, Military, Discovery, Politics, History,
Archaeology, Select, Wharncliffe Local History, Wharncliffe True Crime,
Military Classics, Wharncliffe Transport, Leo Cooper, The Praetorian Press,
Remember When, Seaforth Publishing and Frontline Publishing.

For a complete list of Pen & Sword titles please contact
PEN & SWORD BOOKS LIMITED
47 Church Street, Barnsley, South Yorkshire, S70 2AS, England
E-mail: enquiries@pen-and-sword.co.uk
Website: www.pen-and-sword.co.uk

Contents

About the Author

Gareth Hughes is the Head of History and Head of Lower School at Pocklington School, near York. From 2011-2014 he served as Secondary Education Advisor to the learned body of the British Association for American Studies. He is a sometimes public speaker, conference host and education consultant. Alongside leading school and adult group tours to the battlefields and sites on the Western Front, he has led tours to Normandy, Moscow, St Petersburg, Washington D.C., New York, Alabama, Georgia, Paris, London and Munich. You might also find him, from time to time, serving up banal and trivial comments to the world on Twitter @thehistoryman.

Preface

George Henry Hughes is a name that will mean nothing to you and nor should it. He was my grandfather. In 1916 he found himself in a previously unremarkable area of northern France which I am sure will be familiar to you: the Somme. Unlike the 19,240 on the first day alone who were not so lucky, George survived the battle and the war but spent the rest of his life plagued by ill-health brought on by the wicked toll of shrapnel wounds.

In 1995 I first visited the battlefields of the Great War as a fourteen year old student. The experience was humbling, emotional and ultimately life-changing. It is a pilgrimage that I have subsequently taken every year since becoming a teacher, taking hundreds of students around France and Belgium, both as an accompaniment to their history studies and, more importantly, as a wider aid to their human understanding.

This book is the distillation of some of that experience. It is not meant to be exhaustive, nor even a full tour guide. There are many great sites and memorials that do not make it onto these pages. What it is, however, is the highlight reel.

This book is primarily written for secondary school history departments who wish to undertake a one to three or four day tour of some of the iconic sites of the battlefields of the Western Front. However, it will also be of interest and use to the inexperienced and perhaps first time general visitor to the battlefields. The major focus is on the Somme and Ypres areas, with a few suggestions for those looking to go a little further afield. The book is aimed largely at the non-expert departments (i.e. History Departments who do not specialize in this area/have not taken these trips before or who have previously relied upon tour guides whilst abroad) but will also be useful to those departments which are more confident on the Western Front as a one volume 'pick-up-and-deliver' resource.

Many colleagues I know have felt incredibly daunted when trying to devise their own itinerary and tour due to the huge number of sites and guide books/histories on the market. As the number of these guides has proliferated, so has the miniscule focus on niche areas

of the war. This book is an attempt to strip away that level of detail, all quite brilliant for the battlefield expert but too much for the teacher tour leader, and package a tour of the Western Front that teachers can deliver and students will enjoy.

Therefore, I make no apologies for leaving out details that an expert would deem vital, such as regiments and battalion movements, unless I felt them absolutely necessary in enhancing the understanding of a particular visit for the expected type of audience. This is not meant to be a definitive military history; the main aim is to provide context, narrative and a gripping experience, which will hopefully inspire the individual to carry out reading and research of their own and give them an interest for life.

Quite simply, my hope is that this book gives you all you need to deliver a moving, entertaining and memorable trip.

For the individual visitor this book will enable you to get a good grasp of the key areas and history through a few accessible itineraries for self-touring.

Finally, I must pay my debt to the masters of this genre whose books I hope you will now seek out. If it were not for the outstanding and numerous publications by Major and Mrs Holt, the Battleground Europe series and the magnificent *Before Endeavours Fade* by Rose Coombs then my own ventures across the Western Front would simply not have happened. This book is where you start your journey – their books are where you master it.

Gareth Hughes, Pocklington, February 2014.

The Great War in Numbers

4 years, 4 months, 14 days – duration of the war

64.7 million – men mobilised by all combat nations during the war

35 million – casualties

15 million – dead

634 – Victoria Cross medals awarded

11 – % of French population killed or wounded

7.5 million – soldiers with no known grave

230 – soldiers killed per hour of the war

250,000 – British amputees

91,198 – deaths from gas attacks

185 billion – cost in dollars of the war

720,000 – size of British Army in 1914

5.7 million – men mobilised into British Army by 1918

10,000 – killed, died, wounded or missing on 11 November 1918

How to use this book

In this guide are two main itineraries: the Somme and Ypres. The Somme is a one day itinerary and Ypres a day and a half. I have also provided ideas for another half a day at both locations. There is also a short chapter with a full day itinerary to give an introduction to Mons, Arras, Loos and Neuve Chapelle, if you have the time to do so.

The itineraries give you a realistic amount of visits for a day. The most common mistake for schools and general visitors trying to do their own trip without a tour guide is to cram too much in – it is also the same mistake that enthusiastic and knowledgeable tourists make too. I have certainly had to learn to limit my own itineraries. I have also endeavoured to avoid "cemetery fatigue", which is a particular threat to student groups.

At each site there is information which relates to:

- Context of the location
- Your orientation (where relevant)
- Spiel – the most crucial part! Essentially, the history and stories with which to engage and entertain your charges. Or, for the individual using this guide, the information to help you to understand each visit.
- Activity (where relevant).
- Any relevant photographs and maps. However, I would also recommend purchasing Major and Mrs Holt's Battle Maps of the Somme and the Ypres Salient alongside a good road map.

Along the way there will be tips for lunch breaks, free time for students and other helpful pointers.

Sentences written in italics are directions or instructions to you.

Visiting the Western Front with a School Group

Although this book can be used by the individual traveller, be they first time to the Western Front or a veteran of such ventures, when I originally conceived the idea it was with school groups or groups in general in mind. Therefore, these next few short paragraphs are intended for a teacher leading such a group or anyone leading a group. If you have the good fortune of not being a teacher, or leading a group around the sites, then please do skip this section.

* * *

Why do it?

Well, this question is probably redundant if you have gone to the trouble of buying this book. For value for money, curriculum content, enjoyment and overall impact on the students, you will have trouble finding a better trip.

Which age groups should I take?

The simple answer is any, although I would recommend not younger that Year 9. I have taken mixed groups ranging from 13-18 and GCSE only. I have taken trips which are solely pitched as an 'interest' trip and those which are linked to GCSE coursework. Personally, the freedom of the 'interest' trips, where those students on the trip are there because they already have an interest in the war, makes the venture usually more enjoyable.

How do I go about booking it?

It is a simple conundrum; to tour company or to not tour company? Based in the north of England, I favour using a tour company, simply because they have the ability to get better deals on the ferry crossing than I can usually do and this outweighs the (relatively small) additional costs which they charge in order to make some profit. My trips tend to be relatively long compared to many; five or six days being the norm. However, if I were based in the south and taking a one or two day trip, then it is relatively straightforward to book without a tour company and still obtain good prices on whichever crossing route you favour.

A note on ferry crossings; I know many teachers who fear the overnight crossings. I have done both the short crossing and the overnight ones and by a large margin I prefer the overnight crossing. The students love them and it adds an extra something to the trip as a whole. You just have to be tight on where students are allowed to go (e.g. not outside on deck without a teacher) and on regular meeting up times.

There are many good tour companies out there; best to shop around for the package that suits your particular needs.

The main considerations to make are: how much of the booking process do you feel comfortable handling; and how much of the trip will you lead yourself?

I have never been before – do I need a guide?

You have this book! However, if you cannot get out to France and/or Belgium for a pre-trip recce, so that you can visit the places and get a feel for how to deliver the trip using this book, perhaps use a tour guide on your first trip whilst reading this book along the way. In future years you will be able to take the trip yourself and save on the added cost of hiring guides.

What processes, risk assessments, pre-trip planning requires carrying out?

This will very much depend on your school policies. In general, you will have to seek permission to run the trip, put out letters of interest to the students, reserve your

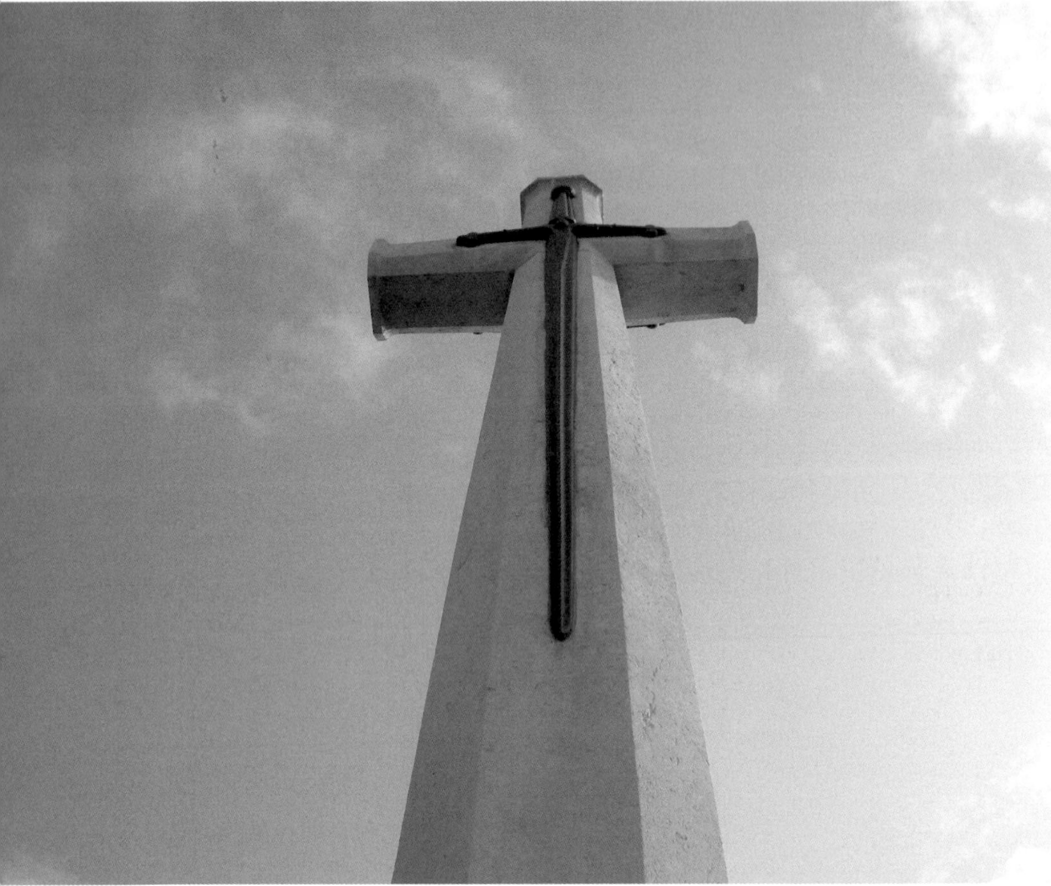

accommodation and travel whilst collecting deposits, fill out risk assessments, collect all monies and host an information evening for parents. However, the first port of call is your Director of Activities/Co-Curriculum/Educational Visits and your school policies. Do not let the paper work put you off; the trip is more than worth it!

Where should I stay with the group?

This really depends on age range and what you wish to do on a night. If you are using a tour company then they can cater to your needs. I have stayed in numerous locations over the years. For younger students I like Château d'Ebblinghem near St Omer, due to its floodlit football pitches and games rooms. However, in recent years I have been converted to the outstanding Menin Gate School Hotels; they are well run and provide everything you require in a brilliant location: www.thepoppies.be. The fact that the accommodation is all yours whilst you are there is a major bonus, as is the fact that your evening meal is always at a good restaurant in Ypres itself. There are, I am certain, many good places to stay – you will find one that works for your particular needs.

Coach Travel

This can make your life easy… or absolute hell. Please, whatever else you do, ask for a driver who knows the Western Front! You have numerous other things to worry about whilst abroad, the last thing you need is to be map reading for someone who has never left the UK before (which has happened to me). Although now fairly common, I would urge you to pay the extra (relatively minor) cost to get a luxury coach (leg room and a toilet).

What should I take with me?

Although I would like to think this book will suffice for leading a tour, your interest is likely to grow over the years and you will want to develop your own unique tour, bringing in new stops along the way. You will probably wish to take a selection of good books with you to help. See the further resources section of this book to get you started.

It is a good idea to take a healthy supply of remembrance crosses with you so that students can leave them at headstones as they wish. If you are taking part in the Last Post Ceremony then you will also require a wreath. Visit http://www.britishlegion.org.uk/ to organise this.

In the last few years I have found the addition of a tablet device extremely useful. On this you can obviously store relevant images of individuals, maps, battle photographs, audio and visual content.

DVDs for the coach are obviously a good idea too.

Any tips?

Start your days early, build in toilet stops and free time, try to limit cemetery visits to four or five a day, if you can, and end at a reasonable time so that the students can relax a little too. If the weather is wet (more often than not you will encounter some rain whilst away) make sure students have brought waterproofs with them and a change of footwear so that muddy boots and a readily identifiable bag to put them in can be left in the coach luggage compartment.

The main point is to be flexible. Too many tour leaders try to stick to their itinerary throughout and ignore the obvious signs when a group starts to flag. Have a few contingency visits up your sleeve and try to build in an overarching theme to each day so that the students have something to grasp on to throughout. It is a good idea for them to have a guide to the trip too, something that they can read on the coach.

I do not tend to go for the worksheet route when visiting sites. This is simply personal preference; I have witnessed several brilliant uses of such material. Ideas for these could be to collate designs of cap badges, follow particular regiments or old boys of the school or for considering unique aspects of the burials in a particular cemetery. You can, of course, make them to fit whatever task you need.

Finally, make sure you build in time for a drink of an evening; you will deserve it! Enjoy.

* * *

3566 PRIVATE
H. C. RICHARDS
7TH BN. AUSTRALIAN
20TH SEPTEMBER 1917
EGIMENT
1914

The British Army

One of the most confusing aspects of the Great War is that of unit sizes within the armies. Below is a simplified look at the composition of the British Army[1]:

Unit/Formation	**Number of Men**	**Commanded by**
Platoon	50-55	Lieutenant/Second Lieutenant
Company	240	Captain/Major
Battalion	1,100	Lieutenant Colonel
Brigade	c.5,000	Brigadier General
Division	15,000-18,000	Major General
Army Corps	36,000-40,000	Lieutenant General
Army	180,000-240,000	General

By late summer 1916, The British Expeditionary force had Five 'Armies'. The discrepancy in numbers in the final three formations is due to how large the support systems were, e.g. artillery, engineers, medical; and the number of corps in a particular Army. The basic reason for the division into units is to streamline command and control. The Americans had divisions of nearly 24,000 men, which proved too cumbersome in the field.

The French and German armies were roughly organised along the same lines.

British regiments are different and confusing. They were essentially an historic designation, such as The Black Watch or The Green Howards, and were incorporated into the breakdown above. A regiment could range from 1,000-80,000 men. The French, German and U.S. armies used regiments as a formation, i.e. a combination of battalions.

Finally, when these units went into battle, they were rarely at full strength. Either due to illness, injury, leave or death, numbers would be depleted. A battalion should, in theory, number 1,000 but a strength of 700 was more the norm.

Footnote:

1. Adapted from Groom W, *A Storm in Flanders*, pxii

The Great War – A Timeline

1914

28 June	Archduke Franz Ferdinand, heir to the throne of the Austro-Hungarian Empire, assassinated by Gavrilo Princip of the Black Hand gang
1-4 August	Declarations of War by the major players
4 August	Germany, putting the Schlieffen Plan into operation, invades Belgium. Britain declares war
7-18 August	The British Expeditionary Force (BEF) arrive on mainland Europe
23 August	The Battle of Mons and the retreat to the Marne begins
26 August	Battle of Tannenberg begins on the Eastern Front
6 September	Allied counter attack on the Marne followed by German retreat. Stalemate
15 September	'Race to the Sea' begins; trenches form along the Western Front
19 October	First Battle of Ypres begins
29 October	Turkey enters the war on the side of the Central Powers
25 December	The famous informal Christmas truce occurred on some sections of the Western Front

1915

1 January	Allied offensive in Artois and Champagne begins
19 January	First zeppelin raids on England
4 February	German U-boat attacks on Allied and neutral shipping and declared blockade of Britain begins
19 February	Allied attack at the Dardanelles and Gallipoli begins
10 March	Battle of Neuve Chapelle begins
11 March	Britain begins blockade of German ports
22 April	Second Battle of Ypres begins; first use on the Western Front of poison gas by Germany
7 May	RMS *Lusitania* is sunk
23 May	Italy enters the war on the Allied side

25 May	Asquith forms a coalition government in Britain
25 September	Battle of Loos. French engage in Champagne offensive
19 December	Sir John French relieved of command; Sir Douglas Haig becomes Commander-in-Chief of the BEF
26 December	Allies begin withdrawal from Gallipoli

1916

21 February	The Battle of Verdun begins
24 April	Easter Rebellion begins in Ireland
31 May	Battle of Jutland
4 June	The Brusilov Offensive begins; Russia come close to total victory over Austria-Hungary. Germany now 'shackled to a corpse'
5 June	T.E. Lawrence leads Arab revolt against the Turks in the Hejaz
1 July	First Day of the Battle of the Somme
27 August	von Falkenhayn relieved of command; Hindenburg and Ludendorff appointed to replace him
31 August	Germany suspends U-boat attacks
15 September	Tanks on the Somme at Battle of Flers-Courcelette
15 October	Germany resumes U-boat attacks
24 October	Fort Douaumont back in French hands at Verdun
18 November	The Battle of the Somme ends
7 December	Asquith government ends; David Lloyd George becomes Prime Minister
12 December	Germany proposes peace
18 December	The Battle of Verdun ends

1917

1 February	German full unrestricted submarine warfare
3 February	USA cuts diplomatic ties with Germany
24 February	Britain pass intercepted Zimmermann Telegram to the USA – details German proposal to Mexico to form an alliance against the USA
12 March	Russian Revolution begins
17 March	Germany withdraw to the Hindenburg Line
6 April	Following the Zimmermann Telegram scandal and resumption of unrestricted submarine warfare, the USA declares war on Germany
9 April	Battle of Arras; Vimy Ridge captured by the Canadian Corps and attached British formations
16 April	French mauled on the Chemin des Dames, part of the Nivelle Offensive. Mutinies follow
7 June	Messines Ridge offensive begins
26 June	First US troops arrive in France
31 July	Third Battle of Ypres begins

4 October	Second Battle of Passchendaele, part of Third Ypres
7 November	Allied Supreme War Council established in order to better co-ordinate Allied action
10 November	Third Battle of Ypres ends
17 November	Armistice between Russia and the Central Powers
20 November	The Battle of Cambrai begins, tanks used en masse
22 December	Russia enters peace negotiations with Germany (Brest-Litovsk)

1918

3 March	Treaty of Brest-Litovsk signed between Russia and Central Powers
21 March	Germany's last gamble begins: Operation Michael, The Kaiser's Offensive
26 March	Foch Commander-in-Chief of the Allied Armies, appointment confirmed on 3 April
9 April	German advance in Ypres
27 May	German advance on the Aisne
15 July	German advance on the Marne
18 July	Foch counter offensive
8 August	Haig commands successful Amiens offensive, Germans driven back to the Hindenburg Line. "Black Day" of the German Army
12 September	The Americans advance in St Mihiel
27 September	Haig's forces break through the Hindenburg Line
3 October	Germany sues for peace
21 October	Germany end unrestricted submarine warfare
27 October	Ludendorff resigns
2 November	Allied assault along the Western Front
3 November	Austrian armistice; German fleet mutinies at Kiel
9 November	The Kaiser abdicates
11 November	BEF advance into Mons, back where they first saw action in 1914. Armistice at 1100

1919

18 January	Start of Paris peace negotiations
28 June	The Treaty of Versailles is signed. The war with Germany is legally over

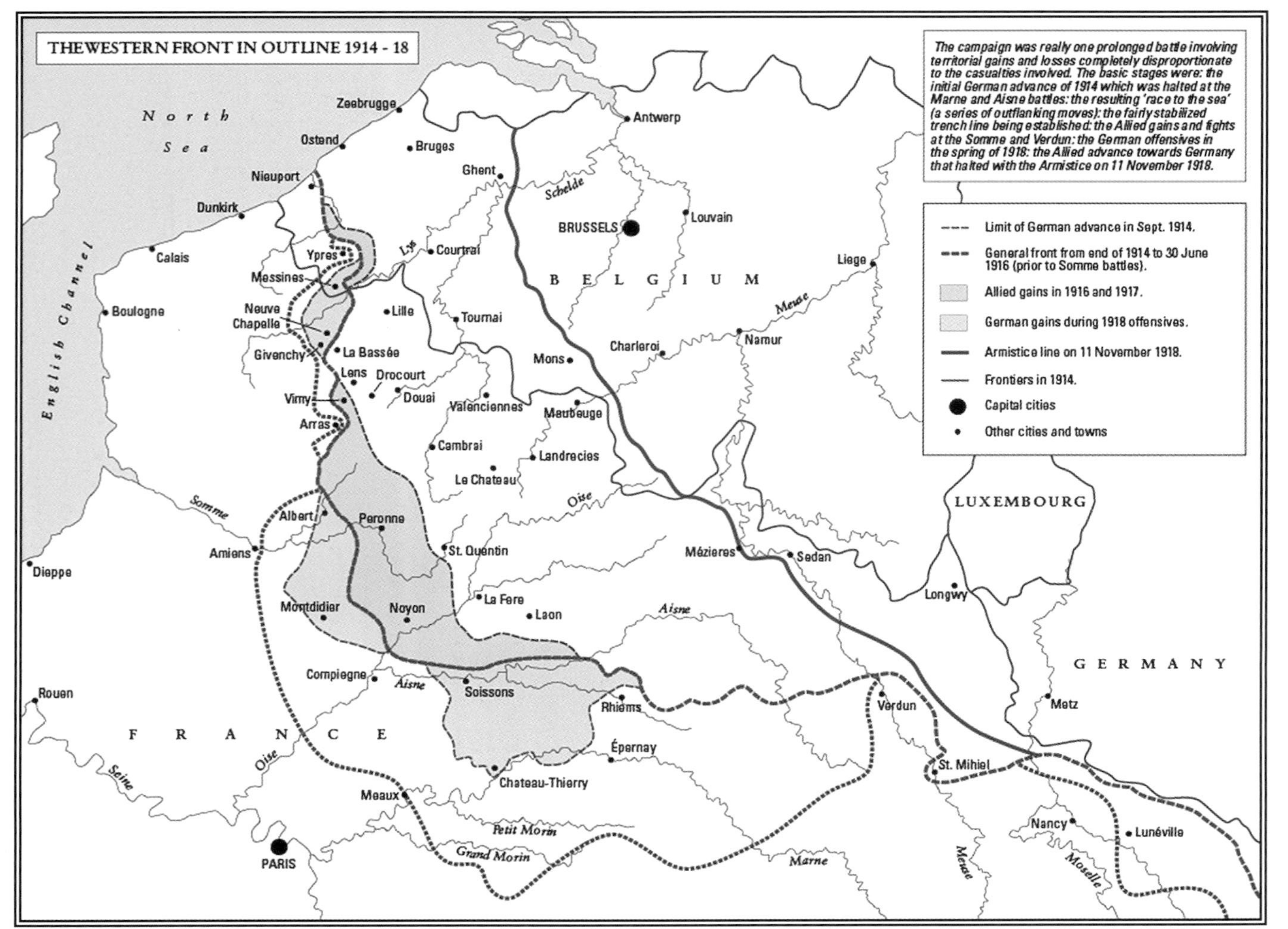
THE WESTERN FRONT IN OUTLINE 1914 - 18
The campaign was really one prolonged battle involving territorial gains and losses completely disproportionate to the casualties involved. The basic stages were: the initial German advance of 1914 which was halted at the Marne and Aisne battles: the resulting 'race to the sea' (a series of outflanking moves): the fairly stabilized trench line being established: the Allied gains and fights at the Somme and Verdun: the German offensives in the spring of 1918: the Allied advance towards Germany that halted with the Armistice on 11 November 1918.
Limit of German advance in Sept. 1914.
General front from end of 1914 to 30 June 1916 (prior to Somme battles).
Allied gains in 1916 and 1917.
German gains during 1918 offensives.
Armistice line on 11 November 1918.
Frontiers in 1914.
Capital cities
Other cities and towns
North Sea
English Channel
BELGIUM
LUXEMBOURG
GERMANY
FRANCE
Zeebrugge
Ostend
Bruges
Nieuport
Dunkirk
Calais
Boulogne
Dieppe
Rouen
Antwerp
Ghent
Schelde
BRUSSELS
Louvain
Liege
Meuse
Namur
Charleroi
Mons
Courtrai
Lys
Tournai
Ypres
Messines
Lille
Neuve Chapelle
Givenchy
La Bassée
Lens
Drocourt
Douai
Vimy
Arras
Valenciennes
Maubeuge
Cambrai
Landrecies
Le Chateau
Oise
Somme
Albert
Peronne
Amiens
St. Quentin
Mézieres
Sedan
Longwy
Montdidier
Noyon
La Fere
Laon
Aisne
Compiegne
Soissons
Rhiems
Verdun
Metz
Épernay
St. Mihiel
Chateau-Thierry
Meaux
Seine
PARIS
Petit Morin
Grand Morin
Marne
Nancy
Lunéville
Moselle

The Great War – A very brief history

Causes

With the annexation of Alsace-Lorraine, following the crushing German victory in the 1870-71 Franco-Prussian war, a future conflagration in Europe was likely. The great statesman, Otto von Bismarck, had been the midwife at the birth of the German Empire, a nation which would rapidly emerge as the greatest industrial and military power in Europe. Following this humiliation, French revanchism became a national rallying cry and would shape not just French military planning but also a people's psyche. The long heralded 'balance of power' on the continent, a concept crucial for the British Empire in maintaining its pre-eminent place in the world, was in a state of turbulent and volatile flux. In the early twentieth century, nationalism, imperialism and militarism bounced around like demented atoms and exponentially increased the likelihood and probable intensity of the next war. Yet, how that war would come was the great unknown.

At the turn of the century, Austria-Hungary was a crumbling and decrepit empire, matched only in decay by that of the Ottoman Turks (a 500 year old power now on its death bed). Both of these wheezing giants edged closer and closer to the new German Empire – Austria-Hungary linked through language, culture and history – but also, much the same as the Ottomans, clinging to the military might of the Germans in their shared fears about the designs and threats of Russia to the east.

Russia, too, faced an uncertain future due to the stirrings of political upheaval by an increasingly agitated proletariat. France longed for war, eager to regain its lost provinces. The French war planning staff, led by Joseph Joffre, had devised a military strategy to suit the French offensive attitude; Plan XVII called for an 'attack at all costs' approach, delivering the French army straight into the heart of Alsace-Lorraine. French tactics were based on two crucial doctrines: one, the *élan vital* - the fighting spirit of the French soldier (the *poilu*), fired by patriotic idealism; two, the offensive *á outrance* - the audacious French soldier moving forward at a rush in order to meet the enemy in close combat and, psychologically speaking, never again to be in a position of national humiliation and defensive desperation. From such planning would emerge the Battle of the Frontiers in 1914, a coordinated invasion of those important lost territories. Across the Channel, it was Great Britain that remained the unknown quantity. The Empire stretched across half of the globe and the Royal Navy maintained its pre-eminent position. Yet, given German ambition, how long could this be maintained?

Germany, led since 1888 by the unstable, jealous and distinctly odd Kaiser Wilhelm II

– a man who over compensated for his own personal physical defects with affected militaristic displays of grandeur – was a European newcomer who was late to the 'Great Game' of imperialism. Jealous of her European rivals' foreign possessions, Germany continued to plan for further war. Should a European war erupt, Germany would strike swiftly and with great precision. Since the 1890s, General Count Alfred von Schlieffen, Chief of the German Great General Staff, had been perfecting a plan to deliver a rapid defeat of France in the west before turning to face Russia in the east. The Schlieffen Plan would be tinkered with, altered and rewritten several times and outlived its author. It would be unleashed in 1914. It was also one of the greatest failures in military history, ensuring that the complete opposite of its objectives would result – a long, stalemate of a war which would lead to the defeat of Germany.

Alliances were the diplomatic trend in the late nineteenth and early twentieth century; designed to ensure parity and a balance of power on the continent, they would, in fact, deliver nothing of the sort. These alliances shifted and fluctuated over time, but by 1914 the delineation was clear. On one side, Germany and Austria-Hungary, to be joined by the Ottomans and other gambling nations along the way, were the 'Central Powers'. France and Russia (also the self-appointed protector of the Slavic people) allied themselves in a defensive partnership, should either be confronted by the Central Powers. Italy, expected to ally with the Central Powers, played the opportunist's game. Belgium remained neutral, with a guarantee of such a position granted in the Treaty of London of 1839, signed by all the great powers, including Great Britain. Finally, in one of the most remarkable realignments in modern history, France and Great Britain had agreed an *Entente Cordiale* in 1904. Although this was little more than an expression of mutual understanding and friendship, in reality it ensured that, for ten years, senior British military figures had been working on the understanding that, should a European conflict emerge, the small regular army of the British Empire would fight alongside France. However, that, by proxy and eventuality, also bound the vast manpower and resources of the British Empire and her Dominions to such a course of action.[1]

So, in 1914, as politicians schemed and military chiefs planned, Europe, even if it did not know it, was on the brink. Who would have expected that love would be the trigger?

Archduke Franz Ferdinand, heir to the throne of Austria-Hungary, had married the Czech Countess, Sophie Chotek, in 1900. However, although a countess, she was regarded of too 'low-birth' for a future Empress. Much to the couple's grievance, she was forbidden from appearing in public with her husband. The Archduke, in an act of love and defiance, knew that if he were to act in his military capacity, as Inspector General of the Imperial forces, then his wife would be permitted to appear alongside him. So, in 1914, on their wedding anniversary, they travelled to a fractious part of the Austro-Hungarian Empire, Bosnia, to inspect the army in Sarajevo. Little did he know that the drumbeat of war was now underway.

Nationalism was rife in the Balkans and was a continuing source of political strife and occasional war. The people of Bosnia-Herzegovina were a mix of Bosnians, Slavs and Croats. A Serbian minority itched to break away and join their homeland.

On 28 June, after already surviving one assassination attempt that day from the Serbian nationalist 'Black Hand' secret society, the Archduke's car took a wrong turning. The driver struggled to operate the unfamiliar gears of the car. At that moment, a young student and member of the 'Black Hand', Gavrilo Princip, stepped out of a café to which he had fled following the failed earlier attempt on the Archduke's life. Given this chance twist in history, Princip raised his pistol and shot dead Franz Ferdinand, Sophie and her unborn child as they sat alongside each other in the rear of the car.

These bullets would lead to the death of millions.

Austria-Hungary, supported by her ally Germany, quickly sought redress. Assuming a Serbian Government plot, they presented her with a list of demands. Nearly frustrating her revenge tainted ambitions, Serbia accepted all but one of the demands – the one failure enough for Austria-Hungary to declare war.

Russia, acting in its paternalistic role to the Slav peoples, mobilized in defence of Serbia. Initially this was a bluff to scare Austria-Hungary but the gamble was checked by the poker playing Germany, which issued an ultimatum to Russia to cease mobilization. Russia refused and on 1 August Germany declared war.

Here was the chance.

The Schlieffen Plan was dusted off and, without any need for a reason, Germany also declared war on France. France, not the least bit concerned by the turn of events, countered with her great plan for national redemption – Plan XVII would now play out its inevitable failures. When the Schlieffen Plan required the German Army to pass through neutral Belgium, in order to by-pass French forces and circle behind Paris in one great pincer movement, the Treaty of London (much to the incredulity of German Chancellor Bethmann-Hollweg, who could not believe that the British would go to war for 'a scrap of paper') was triggered and British troops were destined for the European mainland for the first time in ninety-nine years and not since the defeat of Napoleon. Other nations would be drawn in, some would drop out, Empires would collapse and all would never be quite the same again.

On 3 August 1914, the British Foreign Minister, Sir Edward Grey, stood with a friend in the Foreign Office, looking out on to the streets of London below. Dusk was edging in and the street lamps were being lit. Grey, with an apt melancholy and sense of sharp foreboding, uttered his now much remembered phrase: 'The lamps are going out all over Europe; we shall not see them lit again in our life-time.'

The world was now at war.

The War

1914

On 7 August the first elements of the relatively small British Expeditionary Force (BEF) arrived on the European mainland. Alongside French forces, it first made contact with the German army at Mons in Belgium; then followed the Allied retreat to the Marne. Yet, the German advance had been successfully checked and the Schlieffen Plan was in tatters. Both sides now tried to outflank each other and thus followed the "race to the sea", eventually ending in a series of trench systems spreading from the Swiss border to northern France and Belgium. As both sides began to adapt to the new reality of a defensive and stalemated conflict on the Western Front, the war went global.

In an almost perverse reverse of the Schlieffen Plan, Germany enjoyed early great success on the Eastern Front at the Battle of Tannenberg, which very nearly knocked Russia out of the war completely. War spread to the African colonies and to South America, whilst Japan allied with the Entente (eying German possessions in the region and with long standing territorial ambitions in China) and Turkey joined the Central Powers. The war would not "be over by Christmas", although the festive season was celebrated across a number of sections of the Western Front, as soldiers from both sides left their trenches and met in No Man's Land during an unofficial truce.

1915

Immediate victory had been denied to Germany and initially 1915 did not look promising for her. Italy, in a reversal of pre-war alliances, entered the war on the Allied side. The German Navy was now blockaded in port and thus could offer little help to German colonies and Japan was already overrunning German possessions in the east. Furthermore, the Central Powers were geographically cut off from their ally Turkey. Russia besieged Austria-Hungary but events soon shifted in Germany's favour. In February, Russia endured heavy fighting in The Winter Battle of the Masurian Lakes and retreated out of Prussia. Considerable German advances occurred in the east through April and May, which turned into a rout of Russian forces in the summer. This eventually enabled the Central Powers to overrun Serbia and geographically link up with Turkey and, a new ally, Bulgaria. By September, momentum was with the German led powers.

This was underlined by events on the Western Front. British involvement in the battles of Neuve Chapelle (March), Second Ypres (April-May) and Loos (September-October) were all indecisive and frustrating affairs, which did little beyond underline the difficulty both sides now faced in undertaking any offensive strategy. Heavily fortified defences, barbed wire, heavy artillery, machine guns and gas were the hallmarks of such warfare.

In an attempt to open up another front in the war and end the inertia which had developed in the west, Allied forces attempted an assault on Turkey in the Dardanelles campaign. Despite a nine-month attempt, little was achieved beyond more lost men and on Boxing Day the withdrawal began. This war would have to be won, somehow, on the Western Front. Sir Douglas Haig, the newly appointed Commander of the BEF, would be the man tasked with achieving it for the British.

1916

For many, this was the most vivid and illustrative year of the nature of the war. In February, Germany unleashed a breath taking offensive at the ancient medieval fortified city of Verdun. Using a massive artillery bombardment and strategic attrition, the grim aim was to bleed France white by drawing her forces into defending the position at all costs, knocking her out of the war and thus leaving Britain vulnerable. It became one vast and horrific mincer of men.

Partially in an attempt to relieve the pressure on the French at Verdun, the French and British undertook an offensive on the Somme; 1 July becoming a day synonymous with British military failure. Verdun and the Somme would trudge on until both campaigns were finally put out of their misery in December and November respectively.

At sea, the only major surface naval battle of the war took place when the British and German High Seas Fleets engaged at Jutland in May. Technically, in man power and numbers of ships lost, the Germans triumphed but the German Fleet was so badly damaged that it returned to port and its commanders were so shaken that it was never to re-emerge – thus most regard this as a British victory.

Elsewhere, Lawrence of Arabia led the Arab revolt, the Brusilov Offensive by Russia critically wounded Austria-Hungary, Hindenburg and Ludendorff succeeded Falkenhayn and Lloyd George became British Prime Minister.

1916 was a brutal year and no victory, for either side, was anything like near.

1917

A year of change and upheaval. On the Western Front, Germany carried out a strategic withdrawal to the heavily fortified defensive positions of the Hindenburg line, whilst Allied assaults were carried out at Arras and Ypres in the spring and summer. At Third Ypres (Passchendaele) another large scale attritional attack was carried out, with results depressingly similar to the Somme. Given the horrific weather conditions, much of the fighting was undertaken in an obliterated landscape dominated by glutinous mud, presenting the imagery that most people associate with the war as a whole. However, by the year's end, many new methods were being utilised by the Allies, most noticeably with the mass use of tanks at Cambrai.

Russia, in the midst of the Bolshevik revolution, agreed an armistice with Germany, whilst the French army became mutinous following the very disappointing Nivelle Offensive. It was the necessity to relieve the pressure on the French forces that forced Haig's hand to carry out the ill fated Ypres offensive.

In the Middle East, British forces enjoyed major success and, in general, outside of Europe the Allied forces were seizing the initiative. Following the German decision to carry out unrestricted submarine warfare and with the release of the Zimmerman telegram (a German offer of an alliance with Mexico in the event of war with the USA) to an incredulous American public, the USA entered the war on the Allied side in April. Although it would take months for American forces to arrive in any significant numbers, the potential increase in manpower and resources for the Allies would force Germany to take a gamble for victory in 1918. In a long overdue move, the Allied forces established a co-ordinating policy body, eventually leading to Ferdinand Foch being appointed as overall Supremo. This, combined with the desperation of Germany to end the war as swiftly as possible, meant that the conditions necessary for an Allied victory were finally emerging.

1918

With Russia agreeing terms with Germany in March, German forces were released from the Eastern Front and thus available for a massive assault in the west. Operation Michael, The Kaiser's Offensive, was Germany's last gamble to win the war before the USA's military strength could be felt in the theatre. From spring through to early summer this assault was a success, at least in terms of ground gained. In a foreshadowing of the tactics of the Second World War, German storm troopers moved at pace and thrust the Allies back all along the Western Front – mobile warfare had returned. German troops pushed as far as the outskirts of Paris. But the Germans outran their supply lines and Allied counter offensives from July pushed the German Army into a full retreat. On 8 August (the famous Black Day of the German Army), following Haig's Amiens offensive, the Germans were forced back toward the Hindenburg Line. In late September, the Allies moved through the Hindenburg fortifications and in late October the Germans began to sue for peace. The Allies kept pushing and much of Belgium and France were finally liberated from German occupation.

By early November the Austrians had capitulated, the German home front was gripped by revolutionary fervour and widespread hunger (the Allied blockade having been a major success) and her navy was in mutiny. On 9 November the Kaiser abdicated and left Germany and, with British forces back in Mons where they had begun in 1914, an Armistice was agreed for 1100 on 11 November.

The guns fell silent.

1919

In January the Paris peace negotiations began. On 28 June, five years to the day since Archduke Franz Ferdinand was assassinated, the Treaty of Versailles was signed between the Allies and Germany, thus officially ending the war.

The total number of military and civilian casualties topped 35 million, with over 15 million of these dead.

Twenty years later, war would ravage the world again.

* * *

Footnote:

1. No Dominion had an obligation to provide troops for anything other than its own defence. However, the cry of Mother Britain would be answered by them anyway.

A row of headstones at St Symphorien CWGC Military Cemetery.

Remembrance, Memorialisation and the Commonwealth War Graves Commission

The Commonwealth War Graves Commission (CWGC)

In 1914, a forty five year old director of an international mining company, finding he was too old to join the British Army, became commander of a mobile unit of the British Red Cross on the Western Front. This was Fabian Ware, a remarkable man who is principally responsible for the beautiful cemeteries you see today.

Ware had been deeply troubled in his first months in France by the obvious lack of an official recording process of the soldiers' graves that were beginning to spring up near to the battlefields. Ware set about correcting this and, by 1915, his work with the Red Cross was officially recognised as one of major national importance, being transferred into a new Graves Registration Commission in the British Army. By the end of 1915, agreement was reached with French authorities that land would be granted, in perpetuity, to the British Empire for the burial of the fallen and that the British would maintain the cemeteries.

By 1916, Kew Gardens were supplying seeds and plants for the cemeteries and on 2 May 1917 the body was granted a Royal Charter and named the Imperial War Graves

Commission. In the same year, Ware began registering photographs of graves and graveyards for relatives of the dead.

Once the war ended, the real process of fully registering, recording and memorialising the dead could begin. It was immediately recognised that the importance of these cemeteries, as a symbol of sacrifice and as a place of pilgrimage, would be considerable. In 1960 the commission was renamed the Commonwealth War Graves Commission and in 1964 its charter was extended to include the dead of the Second World War. Today the CWGC is responsible for the graves and memorials of 1.7 million Commonwealth service personnel. Of these, over one million rest in graves, with those unknown remembered on memorial walls. Their work spreads to 153 countries with a full-time workforce of 1,200 people. Their outstanding work ensures that those who lost its lives cannot be forgotten.

The cemeteries

After the war, amidst some heated parliamentary debate, two important principles were established for the cemeteries: first, bodies would not be repatriated due to the scale of the undertaking and the importance of the comrade in arms symbolism; secondly, the headstones would be uniform, so that no distinction would be made in rank or background.

Each headstone displays (if known) the rank, name, regimental number and crest, unit, age and date of death. An inscription could be chosen by the relatives[1] and the choice of a religious emblem. Portland stone was the predominant material used, but today Botticino stone from Italy is preferred due to its durability. The headstones are 2ft 8in high and 1ft 3in wide.

The philosophy was to create tranquil, permanent resting places, with the feel of a British garden, which would inspire reflection and honour the dead. The three main architects tasked with designing and realising these goals in France and Belgium were Sir Edwin Lutyens, Sir Herbert Baker and Sir Reginald Blomfield. The planting schemes were designed by Gertrude Jekyll.

After the death of his son at the Battle of Loos in 1915, Rudyard Kipling joined the Committee overseeing this work. Graves of soldiers whose remains could not be verified bear the inscription 'Known Unto God', which was selected by Kipling. He also suggested the verse from Ecclesiasticus, 'Their Name Liveth for Ever More', for inscription on the Stone of Remembrance, designed by Lutyens, which you will find in the larger cemeteries. In almost all of the burial grounds you will see the Blomfield designed Cross of Sacrifice – the only clearly Christian symbolism.

The iconic portland stone CWGC headstone.

The Stone of Remembrance.

Cross of Sacrifice.

Immediately after the war, as many grieved for their lost loved ones, developing cemeteries and memorials was a hugely sensitive business. Some were against any obvious display of religion whilst many others found that idea horrific. Traversing this was a challenge.

You will likely come across graves which read ‘Believed to be buried in this cemetery’ and ‘Known to be buried in this cemetery’ or ’Buried near this spot’; the former refers to situations where there is an element of doubt whilst the latter two refers to the occasions where cemeteries were either destroyed by subsequent battles in the war (this was especially common when movement returned to the war in 1918) or from moving burials from smaller cemeteries into larger concentration ones and positive identification was an impossibility.

Nearly all of the cemeteries have a small bronze door which contains within both the cemetery register and a visitors book. Please do sign the latter and encourage your students to do the same.

Memorials

In the many instances where bodies were not found (over 300,000 British and Commonwealth soldiers) their names are commemorated on a series of impressive memorials across France and Belgium. The most famous of these are the Lutyens’ designed Thiepval Memorial on the Somme (72,194 names), the Blomfield designed

Panels on the Menin Gate memorial.

Menin Gate (54,382) and Baker's Tyne Cot Memorial (34,916) – the latter two both in the Ypres sector. As and when bodies are found and identified, the names of the soldiers are in due course removed from the memorial.

Visiting a particular grave or memorial panel

If you are wishing to visit the grave of a relative, or locate them on a memorial, then make

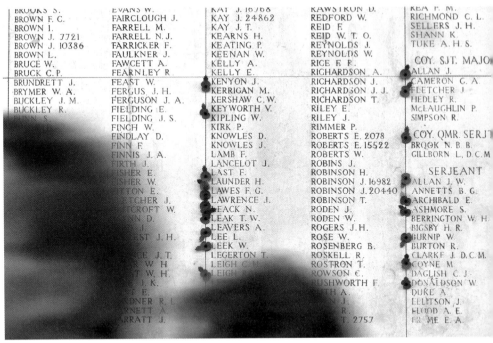

use of the brilliant www.cwgc.org, where you can start your search on the home page. If you have a name, the website will provide you with the cemetery and the plot and row where the grave can be located. For memorial panels, you will be given the panel number. If you do not have full details, or if – as can happen – the official record seems to be incorrect, then contact the CWGC, they will do all they can to help. One other important point: it is a good idea to take a copy of the layout of the cemetery with you to help locate the plot once you arrive. This can be gained from the website too. A copy should be in with the register details at the cemetery, but they can go missing.

Please do inform your students many weeks before you travel that they should find out if they have a relative buried or memorialised in the region. As we move further and further away from the war, many simply do not realize (and sometimes neither do their parents!) and it can take some digging through their family history to find this out. It really can add so much to your visit and make it exponentially more memorable for your students and yourself. I find it necessary to remind the group each time I send a communication home before we travel and I still routinely have the scenario where I am told, on the coach, somewhere in France, that the student does in fact have a relative buried nearby (enter frantic map work to see if I can detour!).

I have been witness to remarkable occurrences, such as when two students found their relatives in the same row of graves and two others found theirs on the same memorial panel. In general, a visit to a relative of somebody on the trip often brings a sense of a shared journey to the group as a whole. It never fails to dampen the eyes.

Footnote:

1. The New Zealand authorities did not grant this option.

The all too common inscription denoting that the grave is that of an unidentified British/Commonwealth soldier.

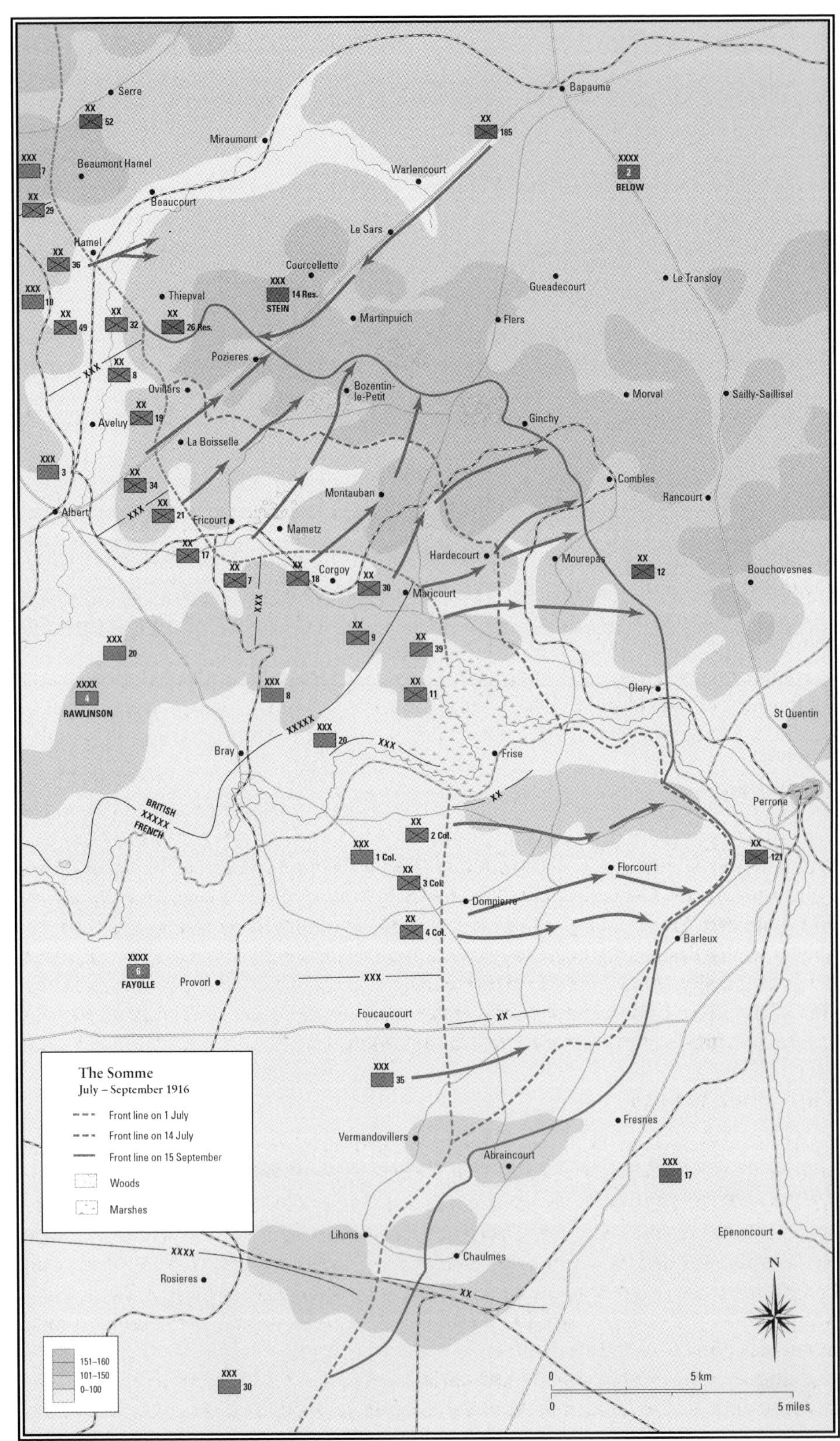

An overview of the Battle of the Somme.

Tour One:
The Somme

If two words in the English language can evoke visions of carnage and heroism, loss and futility, pathos and *history*, then surely none are better than: the Somme.

The Battle of the Somme took place between 1 July and 18 November 1916. More than 1,000,000 soldiers from Britain and her Empire, France and Germany were casualties and it is one of those events in history which has become part of Britain's collective memory. The Somme is one of the most discussed, misunderstood and important occurrences, not just in the war, but also in how mankind developed after it.

A visit to the battlefields of the Somme can be haunting, it is always moving but, more than most other areas of the Western Front, it is a visit which brings alive the conflict. It is, comparatively to Ypres and Arras, quite straight forward to follow the battle lines, walk the footsteps of individual soldiers and enjoy views of battlefield vistas. It is an immediate and illuminating visit. It will bring sense to what, for many, were a senseless few months.

The Prelude

The Allies had agreed a broad strategy for 1916 in early December 1915 at Chantilly. Whilst Russia would attack German forces from the East and Italy opened an offensive against the Austro-Hungarians, French and British forces would launch a major assault on the Western Front. Douglas Haig had wished for this attack to be made in the Ypres Salient, with a desire to break through and capture German held channel ports. However, it was eventually decided that the main campaign would be carried out in France – either side of the River Somme, a previously quiet sector of the front. The original planning was for an attack by forty French divisions and twenty five British over a fifty mile front.

Then came Verdun

On 21 February, a single shell, fired from a 38cm gun, travelled twenty miles and slammed in to the Bishop of Verdun's palace. Ten months later, 37 million more had been fired and 976,000 men had become casualties of the mincer of men that was the gruesome brain-child of General Erich von Falkenhayn. The Battle of Verdun was the longest single battle of the war and its aim was to 'bleed France white' or, simply, to draw as many French troops into the defence of this symbolic ancient fortress town and kill as many as was possible. Falkenhayn hoped to destroy the French Army and then Germany could turn its attention to an isolated Britain.

Verdun is a movingly evocative and terrible story. It deserves far more time than can be apportioned it here. However, the major effect, in the short term, of this German assault was seriously to alter Allied plans for 1916. The entire French Tenth Army was withdrawn from the Somme and sent as reinforcements to Verdun. With French generals and politicians demanding an urgent British attack in the north, in order to draw German forces away from Verdun and relieve pressure on the French, the battle plans for the Somme were redrawn, with the British now the dominant player in the ill-fated game that was about to begin.

It is not entirely clear why an attack on the Somme would be of any great benefit to the Allies, given the obvious difficulty in capturing the German positions, which were on high ground, defended in depth, with deep dugouts as protection and with no obvious strategic objective. However, this was very much a political move with operational considerations a distant second – not much comfort for either the general or the ordinary soldier.

The Plan

The attack would take place over a twenty six mile front, with the British responsible for just short of sixteen of these, stretching from Gommecourt in the north to Maricourt in the south. The French were responsible for the assaults south of Maricourt, with General Sir Henry Rawlinson's Fourth Army carrying out the main advance. The Third Army would carry out a diversionary effort at Gommecourt, in the hope that German forces would be drawn away from Rawlinson's troops to his south.

The plan aimed for an advance of some 4,000 yards on the first day, with the intention of capturing the high ground from Montauban to Serre, taking place after a massive artillery bombardment that would obliterate German defences. This high ground could then act as a good observation point or, even better, from here Rawlinson could pivot the Fourth Army northwards and "roll-up" the German forces, forcing a major, possibly decisive, withdrawal eastward. The cavalry had Bapaume as a objective.

The Somme would be the major debut of Kitchener's New Army. Some of the Pals Battalions first saw action at Loos in 1915. They would bleed far more heavily in 1916.

The Secretary of State for War, Field Marshal Earl Horatio Herbert Kitchener, had been proven entirely correct in his early predictions that the war would be far from brief and it would be one of such carnage that Great Britain would require many more soldiers than were in the regular army at the outbreak of hostilities. Thus Kitchener created a volunteer army, with over 500,000 men answering the call. Whole battalions were formed from men from single towns; football teams joined up together, factory workers downed tools and joined queues, whole streets were seemingly emptied of their young men.

In order to incorporate the new volunteer army, Rawlinson had instructed them to advance in lines or waves of attack in order to maintain cohesion; although there were some differences in application of this at corps and divisional level. The idea that men wandered in straight lines into machine gun fire is a myth; many of the soldiers adapted and took up crouched running and used the battlefield to shield from enemy fire, as best they could. Haig, in fact, had wanted the British to rush the enemy trenches after a brief, surprise, artillery bombardment but he allowed Rawlinson, at the operational level, to make the final decisions; he chose the more measured and deliberate "bite-and-hold" tactics with the waves of infantry attack at its heart. This, alone, should encourage all those who portray Haig as an ignorant buffoon who sent soldiers to certain death because of an inelastic mind and outdated military dogma, to think again. However, one major criticism that can be made is the poor decision to bastardize Haig's plan for a broad offensive with the hope of a cavalry breakthrough with Rawlinson's of a limited attack on a smaller battle front. The result was a broad offensive with limited aims and a significant dilution of artillery fire. The Fourth Army had 1,437 guns at its disposal but only 182 of these were heavy and shell supply was inadequate. Also, as the weather worsened, the bombardment was extended from five to seven days, thus making the dilution complete.

The artillery was charged with two major objectives: destroy the masses of wire in front of the German positions, which were likely to be impassable otherwise, and annihilate German trenches. The British were largely unaware of the German dugouts which, in places, were almost forty feet underground. It was predicted that the advancing infantry would be able to stroll into the German positions; such was the confidence in the intensity of the prelude bombardment.

Battle was scheduled for 25 June. The weather, as it is wont to do, decided otherwise and the attack was eventually to go ahead on 1 July. The British favoured an attack under the cloak of darkness, but the French wished for daylight, so that their artillery had accurate sight of the battlefield. A compromise (always fear the worst) was made and 0730 would be "jumping off" time for the British and 0900 for much of the French attack.

On Saturday, 24 June, a seven day preliminary bombardment of the German lines began. The noise was astonishing.

1 July

A beautiful summer's day

At 0730 the artillery bombardment finally ceased. A series of mines, seventeen in all, were fired underneath German positions, apart from that at Hawthorn Ridge, which had gone off ten minutes earlier. Watches were checked one final time and then the sound of whistles filled the air. The first waves of attack were already in No Man's Land and the second was about to go over the top. These twenty-seven allied divisions were up against sixteen German divisions. With the artillery bombardment and the clear numerical advantage, men left their trenches sure in the fact that this, if anything really can be in war, was to be a resounding victory.

And then the Germans, largely untouched by the artillery bombardment, emerged from the depths of the earth and manned their machine guns and artillery pieces.

By 0830 at least 30,000 British were dead or injured. By 1200, 100,000 had gone over the top. One of the worst disasters in British military history was underway.

However, the Germans had completely underestimated the propensity and ability of the French to launch any attack unconnected to Verdun and, therefore, the French had made good advances in the south. The British XIII Corps had captured Montauban and Mametz but news further north was terrible. The German stronghold at Thiepval had held, and fighting in and around La Boisselle and Serre was turning into a slaughter.

As the glorious summer sun faded into darkness, the stark reality was that almost half of the original British attack force were dead, dying, wounded or a prisoner; 57,470 men.

What had gone so wrong?

Clearly the artillery bombardment had not done what it was supposed to do. The Germans, safely ensconced in their subterranean shelters, had endured a nerve shattering week, as the shells rained down upon them, but there were simply not enough High Explosive shells for the size of the front attacked. The dilution of artillery fire had been a crucial error. The quality of shells, following the 1915 shell scandal, had not really been rectified and many duds were fired. Shrapnel shells were also little use in destroying the barbed wire; if anything, they made matters worse due to the entanglement effect they created. Therefore, when the British left their positions, the German Army was virtually untouched. Add in to this the inexperience of the New Army and disaster was likely. But that, of course, is the beauty of hindsight. Professor Gary Sheffield puts it well when he says: 'The BEF had attempted to run before it could properly walk, and had paid a horrific price in human life as a result'.

But, as Sheffield also points out, the BEF would learn vital lessons from this horrific day that would be key to their eventual victory in 1918. At a strategic level, 1 July had taken the initiative back from the Germans, who were shocked to find that the French could mount a separate attack on the Somme whilst the fighting in Verdun raged on. Also, 1 July was just one day. One awful day that the Germans won. But it was only one day. The battle continued.

After the first day

If the first day belonged to the German Army, then over the following weeks the struggle equalled out, before, arguably, tipping in favour of the Allies.

Furthermore, disproving the line that the British Army was led by incompetents, La Boisselle was captured on 5 July in part by using a clever "Chinese" or diversionary bombardment to the north, coupled with an attack on the real target by two battalions carrying the lightest of equipment.

By 11 July Mametz Wood was taken (but at some cost) by the 38th (Welsh) Division. In another 'wood', this time Delville, the South African Infantry Brigade underwent five days of the most brutal warfare; at one point it is estimated that shells were falling at 400 per minute on the hapless souls trying to hold that position. The Germans threw nine of their very best available battalions in to the mix, but still the South Africans held until, on 20 July, they were relieved. Of the 121 officers and 3,032 men who went into Delville Wood, only 29 and 751 walked out; fewer than 200 of those were in a fit state to fight any longer.

On 15 September, Haig decided to roll the dice and unleash a new weapon of war: the tank. These slow, cumbersome, unreliable monsters, nevertheless had such an effect when they rumbled in to operation between Combles and Martinpuich, that it was clear to Haig that mechanised and mobile warfare was very much the future. Out of the thirty one that managed to cross the German lines (many had broken down before reaching them) only nine operated properly in tandem with the infantry, but hundreds of Germans surrendered on sighting these beasts or simply fled for their lives. Although a success, it was a limited one and now Haig had shown his hand.

On 25 September another big push was attempted by the Allied command and now the Germans realized that holding the Somme position was neither wise nor useful. Again, on 13 November, and much to German surprise and disillusionment, the Fifth Army, under Sir Hubert Gough, launched a massive attack, breaking through the lines at Beaumont.

By 18 November, Haig concluded that, given the winter months ahead, enough had been done and he halted the Battle of the Somme with an overall gain of close to 120 square miles with a maximum six mile penetration. The British and French had suffered at least 600,000 casualties.

The German Army had lost half a million men. One member of the German General Staff called the battle 'the muddy grave of the German Field Army'. As a result of the acute shortage of manpower, particularly after the Somme and the Austro-Hungarian performance in Russia, the German's set about constructing the Hindenburg Line, to which they would retreat in March 1917, thus giving up their positions on the Somme entirely.

Legacy

The Somme stands in the collective public conscience for everything that was wrong with the First World War: extreme loss of life, terrible generals and futility of the highest order. Sir Douglas Haig has certainly fared the worst from this assessment and the bile spewed upon him during the anti-war laced interpretations of the 1960s was particularly corrosive to his reputation. It is fair to say that the majority of the British public view the Somme through the prism of Alan Clark's book *Lions Led by Donkeys,* the musical *Oh! What a Lovely War* and the TV comedy *Blackadder*. None of these offer a particularly useful or accurate insight, apart from that of a cultural study.

I am far from offering a blanket pardon to the British army commanders on the Somme; simply continuing after 1 July is a highly questionable decision. Using the BEF so soon for such a large undertaking and continuing until November also deserves challenge.

However, what is plainly unfair is the argument that soldiers were sent to certain death without means of adaptation – officers on the ground took operational decisions and reacted to the situation. New weapons and clever tactics were also seen. Yet one of the most obvious conclusions to make is that the Somme hardened the BEF, taught the British Army harsh but vital lessons and seriously hurt the Germans, who, by early 1917, were no longer looking like an army that was confident of victory.

If one looks at the cautious revisionism of the late and great Richard Holmes, or the more controversial arguments of Gary Sheffield and Gordon Corrigan, then it is convincing to look at the Somme, as German and French historians do, as part of a much larger perspective of the fighting on the Western Front and where the British learned some of the lessons that would eventually lead to victory. Nigel Cave argues that historians should focus on the transition: before the Somme the British Army was hugely inexperienced, with many of its senior commanders having never fought a major battle since their appointment to their current position, and lacked sufficient material – especially artillery. After the Somme the German army's fighting ability was still very good but the British would get better.

The Somme was awful, bloody and long; but there was little by way of strategic alternative in 1916. The Germans suffered losses that they could ill-afford and they retreated to the Hindenburg Line just months later.

True, the Somme may be the graveyard of idealism, but it was far from futile.

* * *

'Danger, death, shocking escape and firm resolve, went up and down those roads daily and nightly. Our men slept and ate and sweated and dug and died along them after all hardships and in all weathers. On parts of them, no traffic moved, even at night, so that the grass grew high upon them. Presently, they will be quiet country roads again, and tourists will walk at ease, where brave men once ran and dodged and cursed their luck, when the Battle of the Somme was raging.'

John Masefield, *The Old Front Line (1917)*

One-Day Itinerary

Approximate start time of 0900 and end time of 1600.

To get to all of these sites in one day is possible, but requires good pace. All those sites given a letter addition (i.e. 1a, 2a) are, although highly recommended visits, those stops that I would suggest better to leave out if time becomes an issue.

If you would rather take a more leisurely pace and prepare a lighter schedule, then you might only plan to visit the main stops (i.e. 1, 2, 3…) and if you find that you could do with adding another stop or two along the way then bring in the lettered stop closest to your current location (i.e. if you have just visited 4 then go to 4a).

**1. Serre – Serre Road No 3 CWGC Cemetery/
Sheffield Memorial Park/
Railway Hollow CWGC Cemetery**

1a. Serre Road No 2 CWGC Cemetery

2. Newfoundland Memorial Park

2a. Ulster Tower

**3. Connaught CWGC Cemetery/
Mill Road CWGC Cemetery/
Schwaben Redoubt**

4. Thiepval Memorial to the Missing

-LUNCH-

4a. Authuille CWGC Military Cemetery

5. Lochnagar Crater at La Boisselle

5a. Fricourt German Cemetery

6. Devonshire CWGC Cemetery

7. Delville Wood/South African National Memorial

-DAY END-

Serre Road No 3 CWGC Cemetery.

1. Serre – Serre Road No 3 CWGC Cemetery/ Sheffield Memorial Park/ Railway Hollow CWGC Cemetery

***1 hour stop*[1]**

Serre is a small hamlet that can be reached on the D919 out of Puisieux. This is where the tour begins. CWGC signs clearly indicate the above destinations and there is room for a coach to pull up by Serre Road No 1 CWGC Cemetery. Cars/coaches cannot take the dirt track farm road; disembark with care and walk this path. You are walking from German positions into No Man's Land, which is where you will find your first stop:

Serre Road No 3.

Context

Cemetery in No Man's Land containing graves from 1 July. A good place to set the context for the entire day.

Orientation

You are standing, just, in No-Man's Land. You have walked from the German front-line positions. From here you can see the British jumping-off points down at Sheffield Memorial Park and, due to the dog-leg in the line, the dirt track outside the cemetery was also a British front-line position.

Spiel

If this is the first stop on the first day of your tour:

- Give a short version of the overview history of the war (page 25)

For all tours:

Give an overview of the Battle of the Somme, with particular focus on 1 July (page 37)

Then:

This is Serre Road No 3 Cemetery. It contains eighty-one burials, the majority of which are West Yorks from 1 July 1916. They fell near here. They are forever in No Man's Land.

If this is the first stop on the first day of your tour:

- Give an overview of the work of the Commonwealth War Graves Commission and explanation of the design and commemorations that the group will see (page 31).

Walking towards Sheffield Memorial Park.

Leave the cemetery and continue on the track towards Sheffield Memorial Park. Enter the park and gather your group in what remains of the front line trench, looking back up towards No Man's Land.

Context

Preserved area of front line trenches from 1 July and numerous shell holes.

Orientation

Looking from inside the park towards Serre No 3 or Queen's CWGC Cemetery, you are looking towards No Man's Land and German positions.

Spiel

If, during the course of your visit to the Western Front, you are to stand in a position and truly live history, then this is that place. You are standing in what remains of a front line trench in the British line from 1 July 1916. This is the view that those men, however briefly, would see on that day.

This stretch of the line was made up of men from the 31st Division. These were Pals Battalions; men who volunteered for Kitchener's New Army. All but two of the twelve battalions in the 31st Division were from Yorkshire. This preserved section of the front is named Sheffield Memorial Park after the 12/York and Lancaster Regiment, the Sheffield City Battalion. The 11th Battalion East Lancashire Regiment, also left their trenches on 1 July from this section of the line. Memorials to these battalions, and to many others of the 31st Division who all fought in this vicinity, can be found in this park. For example, the memorial to the Accrington Pals is built out of red iron NORI brick – a brick made in Accrington. It was thought that putting the inexperienced Pals Battalions in this stretch of the line was no risk at all – remember, the artillery bombardment was supposed to have cleared the enemy from the face of the earth. Kitchener's recruits should have been able to stroll across No Man's Land, occupy the German positions and wheel left to roll up and push north.[2] These men were not ready for the reality.

On 1 July, thousands of men stood waiting for the whistle to sound at 0730. In this sector, the most northerly sector of the Somme attack – apart from the diversionary one at Gommecourt – the immediate aim was to break through and capture the village of Serre, a few hundred yards beyond the German front line positions.

What is particularly stark when looking out from here is the realisation of just how exposed the British position was. German machine guns were sited just on the lip of the shallow, but tactically vital, rise ahead. When men left this trench, they could easily be seen by German gunners.[3]

Serre is a fine example of the failures associated with the first day. In preparation for the assault, men dug tunnels out towards the German positions in an attempt to edge

That iconic view from Sheffield Memorial Park toward No Man's Land.

nearer to the enemy front-line and to provide instant communication trenches. Some of these had been located and destroyed by the Germans. Therefore, instead, British troops had cut routes through the barbed wire in No Man's Land and laid white tape to act as direction pointers for advancing soldiers. Much of the tape had simply blown away by the morning of 1 July or acted as a convenient target for German gunners to aim upon, in effect meaning that advancing soldiers would traverse a tunnel of death.

The artillery had failed to make an impact on the German positions and, due to it being partially lifted ten minutes prior to jumping off time, the Germans were ready at their posts by 0730.

When the men left this trench, history would deal them a cruel hand:

> 'There was no lingering about when zero hour came. Our platoon officer blew his whistle and he was the first up the scaling ladder, with his revolver in one hand and a cigarette in the other. "Come on, boys," he said, and up he went. We went up after him one at a time. I never saw the officer again. His name is on the memorial to the missing which they built after the war at Thiepval. He was only young but he was a very brave man.'
>
> \- Private George Morgan, 1st Bradford Pals

As one German machine gunner noted: 'The officers were in the front. I noticed one of them walking calmly carrying a walking stick. When we started firing we just had to load and reload. They went down in their hundreds. You didn't have to aim, we just fired into them.'

The attack by the 31st Division was chaotic, brave (some of the Accrington Pals actually made it to Serre) but, ultimately, a terrible failure. Of 720 Accrington Pals who went over the top, 584 were casualties. The 31st Division lost just over 3,500 men.

Many of those men only managed to walk a few steps into No Man's Land. The gravestones you see ahead of you mark the points where many of those buried actually fell.

George Coppard described what he saw on the morning of 2 July:

> 'Quite as many died on the enemy wire as on the ground, like fish caught in the net. They hung there in grotesque postures. Some looked as though they were praying; they had died on their knees and the wire had prevented their fall. From the way the dead were equally spread out, whether on the wire or lying in front of it, it was clear that there were no gaps in the wire at the time of the attack.
>
> Concentrated machine gun fire from sufficient guns to command every inch of the wire, had done its terrible work. The Germans must have been reinforcing the wire for months. It was so dense that daylight could barely be seen through it. Through the glasses it looked a black mass. The German faith in massed wire had paid off.'

The future Poet Laureate, John Masefield, visited the Somme battlefields one year after it had ended. His account, *The Old Front Line,* is an evocative classic. In these lines, he sums up the final moments of countless men in that war as they left their trenches to attack the enemy:

> '...for one wild confused moment they knew that they were running towards that

Sheffield Memorial Park.

unknown land, which they could still see in the dust ahead. For a moment, they saw the parapet with the wire in front of it, and began, as they ran, to pick out in their minds a path in that wire. Then, too often, to many of them, the grass that they were crossing flew up in shards and sods and gleams of fire from the enemy shells, and those runners never reached that wire, but saw, perhaps, a flash, and the earth rushing nearer, and grasses against the sky, and then saw nothing more at all, for ever and for ever and for ever.'

Activities

Explore the park and read the memorials. Feel free to wander through the shell holes. Railway Hollow CWGC cemetery is at the bottom of the park. It is so named because a small gauge railway line in the valley bottom brought supplies to the troops here. Nearby are Queen's and Luke Copse Cemetery.

I would urge all to fix in their mind that view looking out of what was the front line trench. It is etched in my memory; a view of a small part of the world, soaked in history.

Looking toward Railway Hollow CWGC Cemetery in Sheffield Memorial Park.

1a. Serre Road No 2 CWGC Cemetery

20 minutes

Return to your transport. Serre No 2 is just a little further along the road on your left hand-side. If you are going to visit this stop, then it can be a good idea to tell the coach driver that you will meet him there and walk there with the group, thus eliminating the coach boarding for such a brief journey. You will pass the French Cemetery on the way. Be aware, however, that cars drive at quite astonishing speeds on this road!

Context

Largest British cemetery on the Somme.[4]

Orientation

This is partially on the site of a German stronghold, known as Quadrilateral Redoubt.

Spiel

This is Serre Road No 2 CWGC British Cemetery. It was designed by Sir Edwin Lutyens and was partially built on the site of a German stronghold position called the Quadrilateral

Serre Road No 2 CWGC Cemetery.

Redoubt. There are 7,127 British Graves, 4,944 of which are unknown. There are also thirteen German graves. It is a concentration cemetery and was kept open after the war for burials of newly found remains.

In the field adjacent to this cemetery, towards Serre (not far from the cross memorial to Lieutenant Val Braithwaite), was where it is thought Wilfred Owen witnessed the event which inspired him to write one of his most famous poems, *The Sentry*:

We'd found an old Boche dug-out, and he knew,
And gave us hell, for shell on frantic shell
Hammered on top, but never quite burst through.
Rain, guttering down in waterfalls of slime

Kept slush waist high, that rising hour by hour,
Choked up the steps too thick with clay to climb.
What murk of air remained stank old, and sour
With fumes of whizz-bangs, and the smell of men
Who'd lived there years, and left their curse in the den,
If not their corpses...

...There we herded from the blast
Of whizz-bangs, but one found our door at last.
Buffeting eyes and breath, snuffing the candles.
And thud! flump! thud! down the steep steps came thumping
And splashing in the flood, deluging muck —

The sentry's body; then his rifle, handles
Of old Boche bombs, and mud in ruck on ruck.
We dredged him up, for killed, until he whined
"O sir, my eyes — I'm blind — I'm blind, I'm blind!"
Coaxing, I held a flame against his lids
And said if he could see the least blurred light
He was not blind; in time he'd get all right.
"I can't," he sobbed. Eyeballs, huge-bulged like squids
Watch my dreams still; but I forgot him there
In posting next for duty, and sending a scout
To beg a stretcher somewhere, and floundering about
To other posts under the shrieking air.
Those other wretches, how they bled and spewed,
And one who would have drowned himself for good, —

I try not to remember these things now.
Let dread hark back for one word only: how
Half-listening to that sentry's moans and jumps,
And the wild chattering of his broken teeth,
Renewed most horribly whenever crumps
Pummelled the roof and slogged the air beneath —

Through the dense din, I say, we heard him shout
"I see your lights!" But ours had long died out.

Activity

Walk the cemetery. It might be a good time to ask your group to consider how the German graves are distinguished from the British ones.

2. Newfoundland Memorial Park

1 to 2 hours

It is currently possible to book ahead (email: beaumonthamel.memorial@vac-acc.gc.ca) for a group tour (you must stick to the time given); you *might* be accommodated on the day, but this is unlikely. During the centenary years, because of numbers, the system might change to stands, where different guides explain the significance of a particular point. NOTE that a very good self guided tour (with map) is available from the Centre; relevant stands are marked by wooden posts on the circuit.

http://www.somme-battlefields.com for further information on the Somme sites.

In wet conditions the site might be closed below the Danger Tree, though an alternative (and considerably lengthier route) to the German lines would be available.

Continue on the D919 until you come to a major left turning, the D174, toward Auchonvillers. Keep going until you come to a T-junction. Turn right and then take the left onto Rue Delattre, the D73. Keep on this road for approximately 1.5km and parking is on the right.

Context

Canadian Historic Site and Monument and one of the most tragic episodes of 1 July.

Orientation

You will enter the park and be in the Newfoundlanders' positions, on the left; on the right are those of the Essex Regiment.

Spiel

The village of Beaumont-Hamel was attacked by the 29th Division on 1 July 1916. Overall, this assault would be a failure and the position remained in German hands until 13 November. Where we are now stands as a particular beacon of tragedy for that day.

The 29th Division contained within it the 1st Battalion of the Newfoundland Regiment. Newfoundland is today part of Canada, but on the outbreak of the war she was a Dominion of the British Empire. Men volunteered for service and, after training in the United Kingdom, a battalion of 1,000 soldiers was deployed and first saw action at Gallipoli in September 1915 serving with the 29th Division. With the close of that action, they were moved to the Western Front. On 1 July, they were here.

At 0720 on 1 July, a 40,000lb mine was blown under the German strongpoint at

Hawthorn Ridge. Although it destroyed the strongpoint, it alerted the Germans to the attack which would follow this explosion. At 0730, when the first wave of attack by the 29th Division left their front line trenches, German defenders were already at their machine gun posts. The crater itself would not be captured. Troops of 86 and 87 Brigades were largely stopped in their tracks. The attack was floundering.

The Newfoundlanders were in a support trench, St John's Road (the trench immediately on your left and right as you enter the site), when the attack began. At 0845 they received their orders to advance forward. As they attempted to move to the front line trenches, it soon became apparent that this would be a futile task – the trench system was being bombarded with artillery and was stuffed full of the dead and dying. Congestion and confusion reigned.

They were given orders to leave the trench system and advance from their current positions. They left the trenches. As soon as they advanced over the crest they were clearly visible to the German machine-gunners, who now opened fire at will. Many of the Newfoundlanders never even made it to their own front line. Numerous of the dead were found at the Danger Tree, which you can see in this preserved battlefield site today. Of the 810 (or so, there is some dispute on the accurate figure) men who went into battle wearing the insignia of the Newfoundland Regiment that day, it is estimated that 686 of them were killed or casualties. The battalion was shattered.

Today, the Caribou, emblem of the Regiment, mourns over Newfoundland's fallen youth as it surveys the battlefield. From here you can work your way to the German positions and get an excellent feel for the overall battlefield. Remember what happened here; it is a sacred place.

The great battlefield tour guide, Rose Coombs, wrote about a visit to this site:

> 'It was late July and, as I wandered across the shell-torn slopes towards the German lines, the sound of thunder was heard in the distance, getting gradually nearer as might an artillery barrage. The light grew dim and black clouds gathered overhead. Lightning streaked across the sky – a veritable reincarnation of what a barrage must have been like. As the rain drops began to fall, I dived into one of the trenches for cover and tripped and stumbled along until I found better shelter close to the great Caribou monument which stands guard over the park from a raised mound above a dugout. All the light I had was a tiny torch and this gave little help in avoiding the occasional shell-case or jagged pieces of iron which litter the trenches. After the hot day, the usual smell of rain-soaked grass began to permeate my nostrils . . . but with a difference . . . I realised that this was the smell of battle.'

Activities

This is a large site and takes some time to fully explore and appreciate. There are several cemeteries and monuments as well as the battlefield walk itself. If you have a full guided tour then you will easily be here over 1.5 hours. You could look to the ridge beyond the immediate battle site: below this is where most of the effective German machine-gun fire would have emanated. It is also interesting to note that the effective range of a machine gun was up to c.3000 metres.

The Ulster Tower.

2a. Ulster Tower

10-30 minutes

Continue on the D73 until you come to a T-junction. Turn left. Keep going until you come to a right hand turning over a railway line – take that turn. After just under one km the Tower will appear on your left.

Context

The memorial to the men of the 36th (Ulster) Division.

Orientation

With your back to the tower, looking at the road, German positions were behind you and British in front. At this point, the road is actually in the middle of No Man's Land. In front of you and to your left is the famous Thiepval Wood, which will be discussed at the next stop.

Spiel

The 36th (Ulster) Division enjoyed some of the only success of 1 July encounters north of La Boisselle. They charged out of Thiepval Wood and swept up the incline to our left [*stood with your back to the Tower*] and, beyond the cemetery that you can see on top of the hill, toward an infamous German stronghold: the Schwaben Redoubt. We will also pick up that story at our next stop.

This is the Ulster Tower and is a memorial to those men. It is a replica of Helen's Tower in County Down where the men of the Division trained.

Activities

Point out the orientation and have a look inside the tower and in the grounds at the various artefacts and memorials. There is a small shop, museum and café inside. As you leave the Tower, to your right is a small track into the fields. If you follow the track for about a hundred metres you will find the remains of a German observation post; it is probably part of what was known as the Pope's Nose – another German strongpoint.

3. Connaught CWGC Cemetery/ Mill Road CWGC Cemetery/ Schwaben Redoubt

45 minutes

Connaught cemetery is just past Ulster Tower, on the right hand side of the road.

Connaught CWGC Cemetery

Context

Thiepval wood is behind this cemetery and it was from here that the 36th (Ulster) Division launched their attack on the German lines. There is a section of excavated trench in the wood which can be visited through prior arrangement with the staff at the Ulster Tower.

Orientation

With the wood behind you, look up the crest in front toward Mill Road Cemetery. This is the line of attack that the Ulstermen took on 1 July.

Spiel

Gather at the back of the cemetery

This is Connaught Cemetery and there are 1,268 burials here. Most are men who died on the Somme and many of them are members of the 36th (Ulster) Division. We are going to follow their story on 1 July.

The German Army had held Thiepval and the surrounding areas since September 1914. On 1 July, the Ulstermen were given the task of launching an attack from Thiepval Wood, which is behind this cemetery, and heading up the crest that you see in front of you, to attempt to capture the German stronghold of the Schwaben Redoubt, which was beyond and to the right of the cemetery that you can see towards the top of the hill.

Ultimately, the Ulster Division would be one of the few British relative success stories on 1 July, as they charged the Schwaben, entered its trench and dug out systems, and some even made it to the second line of defences, Stuff Redoubt. However, as we shall see, this gain was temporary and had to be given up due to the failure of forces on either side of this section of the line, as well as the effectiveness of the German counter attack measures.

However, before we walk the footsteps of the Division, the heroism of Billy McFadzean deserves mention. He was in an assembly trench in the wood behind this cemetery, just hours before 0730 on 1 July 1916. In one of the finest books written about the Somme, *The First Day on the Somme*, Martin Middlebrook tells Billy's story. McFadzean was a bomber and, as zero hour approached, he was opening boxes of grenades and passing them around the men. German shelling was quite heavy. 'Suddenly, a box of grenades fell to the floor of the trench [...] the fall had knocked the pins out of two grenades. In four seconds they would explode.' In one of the most remarkable split-second decisions that any man could ever take, Billy McFadzean threw himself onto the fallen and now live grenades:

> 'A moment later the live grenades exploded and Billy McFadzean was dead. In giving his own life, he had saved his friends [...] The shocked Ulstermen laid the shattered body carefully aside, hoping that someone would be able to bury it later, then they finished sharing out the grenades and sadly waited for the battle to begin.[5]

July 1, using the old calendar, was the anniversary of the Battle of the Boyne, and the proud Ulstermen had worked themselves into a religious and nationalistic frenzy.

Just before 0730, the first battalions to attack had left the front line trench system and were positioned in No Man's Land, nearer the German positions. At zero hour, they jumped up and, ignoring the cautious advances witnessed in other areas of the attack, rushed the German trenches. Profiting from the cumbersome German response, they captured the trench and turned their attentions to capturing the Schwaben Redoubt.

We will now walk in the direction of their attack, passing where they once lay in No Man's Land and toward the front line trench that they captured.

Leave the cemetery, cross the road and take the rubble track up to Mill Road CWGC Cemetery.

Mill Road CWGC Cemetery/Schwaben Redoubt

Context

A unique cemetery on the Somme due to the positioning of some of the headstones [explained below]. It is also situated on what was an entrance to part of the Schwaben Redoubt.

Orientation

You have just walked part of the Ulster line of attack. Although you are at a connection to it, the Schwaben stronghold itself was situated north-east of this spot, approximately 200 metres away in the field behind the cemetery.

Spiel

This is Mill Road Cemetery; there are 1,304 burials here. You will notice something rare about this cemetery: several headstones are laid flat. This is because of the terrible subsistence in the area caused by the considerable tunnelling and trench networks; laying the stones flat spreads the weight. It is almost certainly the case that where the headstones are flat mark an incline to the German stronghold.

The Schwaben was one of the most formidable German positions on the Somme; it was a group of linking trenches, underground bunkers, machine gun posts, aid posts, communication areas and a handful of tunnels. It provided an all-round defensive system. This is what the Ulstermen were aiming for.

We left the Ulstermen having captured the front-line trench; we shall pick up their story as they headed for the Schwaben itself.

The Germans in the Schwaben had had time to get out of their underground cover and were ready for the Ulster Division. The Irish, advancing from the captured trench, came under fire from machine gun crews from Thiepval village, the other side of the Ancre and also from hidden snipers. Once in the Schwaben the combat was medieval, raw and bloody. Artillery obliterated men; grenades ripped away limbs and bayonets did their eviscerating best at extremely close quarters. Men's heads were caved in by the butt of a rifle and one man, Captain Eric Bell, won the Victoria Cross for throwing trench mortars (an unbelievable feat, given their weight) at the enemy; these Ulster men were fighting for their lives whilst in such a heightened state of emotion that is near impossible to understand, unless one was there.

The Ulster Division captured the whole of the Schwaben Redoubt and took over 500 German prisoners. Yet now they faced a new set of problems. They lacked command on the ground, its brigade north of the Ancre and the division on the left had both failed – thus leaving the Ulstermen in a salient – and now the German artillery shells began to rain down upon their former stronghold. The Germans began their counter attack.

Later that afternoon, attempts to send reinforcements proved impossible. Men from the 49th (West Riding) Division attempted to cross No Man's Land but were being ripped into by German machine guns from their strongpoints to the east, north and south, as well as artillery fire.

By nightfall the Ulster Division was in an appalling position. No reinforcements had made it through to them and they were desperately short of ammunition. An order was given to retreat. Their heroism was undoubted but their gains had largely been abandoned – at the cost of over 5,000 casualties.[6]

The Redoubt was finally captured on 14 October.

Writing in 1917, John Masefield walked up Mill Road and to the Schwaben. He describes a scene 'littered with relics of our charges, mouldy packs, old shattered scabbards, rifles, bayonets, helmets curled, torn, rolled and starred, clips of cartridges, and very many graves.' When he reached the Schwaben he saw 'nothing whole, nor alive, nor clean, in all its extent; it is a place of ruin and death'.

Masefield also recounts one of the most bizarre stories of the battle, if not the war as a whole; that of a woman, spotted by British soldiers, who appeared on the front of the Schwaben, walking along its edge during a lull in the firing toward it. It was thought that this was a German dressed as a woman (although why they would risk their lives doing this, one could not imagine) but when the British finally took the strongpoint, astonished, they actually found her body and buried her. Therefore, if this is true, then her body lies unmarked somewhere nearby.

It had been a hell of a fight on 1 July; it had been simply hell for many. Yet, had a significant number of reinforcing troops made it through to assist the Ulstermen, to exploit their achievement in taking the Schwaben, it might just have been possible to attack the German positions at Thiepval itself from the rear. This could have completely changed the course of the day and, possibly, the battle overall. 1 July might have been remembered very differently indeed. On the other hand, the Germans had a brilliant counter attack plan.

Return to your transport

The Thiepval Memorial to the Missing.

4. The Thiepval Memorial to the Missing

1/1.5 hours

You will be able to see the Thiepval Memorial on the hill in the distance from the Ulster Tower/Mill Road. Follow on the road until you come to a crossroads and take the right turning. However, the memorial is clearly signed throughout the area.

This is an ideal lunch time spot. There is a seating area and bins which can be found by going up the ramp next to the entrance to the visitors' centre.

The visitors' centre itself is well worth spending time in. The information panels do a great job of explaining the war fully in a simple but unpatronising way.

Context

The memorial to the British and South African men who died on the Somme between 1915 and February 1918 and who have no known grave.

Orientation

Thiepval was a strongly fortified village in German possession. The cellars of houses provided good shelter from the pre battle bombardment in 1916. It was not far from here that machine guns were able to hold up reinforcements getting through to the Ulster Division at the Schwaben Redoubt. The village itself held out on 1 July.

Spiel

This is the Thiepval Memorial to the Missing. It is the largest British memorial to the

A great example of the beautiful arches that make the Thiepval Memorial so unique.

missing in the world. On it are inscribed the names of 72,195 men whose bodies were never found and who died on the Somme between July 1915 and March 1918. Over 90 per cent of those listed here died in the 1916 Battle of the Somme.

This memorial was designed by Sir Edwin Lutyens, who is famed for the Cenotaph in London, many government buildings in New Delhi, India, and is one of the three men responsible for the design of the majority of the cemeteries across the Western Front.

This monument is imposing, captivating and moving. It is made up of interlocking arches, which mean that from whatever angle you view the structure, you should see an arch. It dominates the battlefield around and serves as a fitting tribute to those who lost their lives fighting in this most important of areas.

One point that always reminds you of the continuing relevance and importance of the war is the fact that as bodies are discovered and identified, and they still are, every year, if the soldier's name was listed on this memorial, it is removed – you will be able to spot this. They have been found; they have come home. The rest of these men wait here; we are here to honour them.

Activities

Visitors spend a long time here, searching for names or simply taking in the monument and the history. You may well have a relative to locate. If not, perhaps you could find Billy McFadzean or the composer George Butterworth, whose music is associated with the war and often plays in the visitors' centre. Use the register or computers to locate the panels. The joint Anglo-French cemetery at the rear of the Memorial represents the joint sacrifice of the two nations and their bonds of friendship. The bodies were found along the Western Front in the period immediately before the dedication of the Memorial in 1932.

4a. Authuille CWGC Military Cemetery

15 minutes

Leave the memorial, heading south-west on the D151. You will come to the village of Authuille after 1.5km. The cemetery is signposted.

This visit works best if you are able to play the song The Green Fields of France *whilst visiting.*

Context

Inspiration for a moving song.

Orientation

n/a

Spiel

In 1976, the folk singer Eric Bogle carried out a tour of the Western Front, visiting the sites and cemeteries, much as you have been doing. The story goes that, overcome by the emotion and impact of the day, he sat down next to a grave and began to pen a song. That song was about the grave of a young soldier named Willie McBride. Amazingly, two W. McBride's are buried in this cemetery and at least another twelve died during the war. Given that song writers have artistic licence, there is much debate because the details in the song do not exactly match any of the W. McBrides. However, it is almost certainly the case that the Willie McBride that inspired Bogle was the one buried here in Grave A. 36. The song is a wonderful anthem to the fallen and deeply evocative, whilst also hitting out at the madness of war.

Almost certainly* the *Willie McBride.

Activity

This very much depends on what you feel comfortable with. When the cemetery has been empty of other visitors (as it nearly always is) I have taken a small MP3 player or tablet device and played the song whilst the group gather around the grave. I always find this deeply emotional. However, I do understand that some people may not want to break the tranquillity and listening to the song in your car or on the coach works well too. There are many versions of this song and its name also changes from artist to artist. It can be called *No Man's Land, Willie McBride* or *The Green Fields of France*. My personal favourite version is *The Green Fields of France* by the Irish-Boston band, The Dropkick Murphys.

5. Lochnagar Crater at La Boisselle

30 minutes

Leave Authuille, heading south on the D151. After 2km take the left on to the D20. After a further 2km turn right onto the D929 and then left on the D20. After 400m turn right onto Route de Bécourt and then left on to Route de la Grande Mine.

NB: There is space for coach, but parking is limited.

Context

Largest publically accessible mine crater on the Western Front.

Orientation

Stand with your back to the car/coach parking area. This vast crater is the result of a British mine being blown under a German position, hence you are standing in a German front line trench section. As you look ahead into the farmland and fields you are looking toward the Tara-Usna line, approximately half a mile away; this was the British position behind their front-line trenches, but it is from where Tyneside Irish units of the 34th Division would attack on 1 July. The Albert-Bapaume road roughly cuts straight through the middle of it. To your left is Sausage Valley, so named because of the large German observation balloons that often hung above it, and – of course – it was only proper to name the valley to your right Mash Valley. Avoca Valley is in between Sausage and Mash but further back from them.

Spiel

This is the Lochnagar Crater at La Boisselle; it is the largest accessible crater on the Western Front and was one of seventeen mines blown at 0728 on 1 July 1916 prior to the infantry attack. This mine marks the position of the German front line and for some months men of the British 185 Tunnelling Company had dug from their positions to lay explosives underneath the German trenches. 60,000lbs of explosives were laid.

In general, there were three main aims when planning and carrying out huge mine explosions such as this: destroy dugouts and bunkers; cause mass confusion and disrupt

The mighty Lochnagar Crater.

command and control; create a strongpoint for your own infantry to capture. That a mine would also kill scores of your enemy was a given. It was also hoped, as a fortuitous by-product of the Somme region's geology, that the dust and debris from the blown chalk earth would hang in the air, acting as a useful screen to cover the infantry attack; I have not been able to locate much evidence to support this last point actually occurring.

So, on 1 July at 0728 the crater you see today was blown. Cecil Lewis, then a young officer in the Royal Flying Corps, was flying high above this position and witnessed the explosion:

> 'The whole earth heaved and flashed, a tremendous and magnificent column rose up in the sky. There was an ear-splitting roar drowning all the guns, flinging the machine sideways in the repercussing air. The earth column rose higher and higher to almost 4,000 feet. There it hung, or seemed to hang, for a moment in the air, like the silhouette of some great cypress tree, then fell away in a widening cone of dust and debris.'

The hole was 300ft wide and 90ft deep. It is estimated that nine German dugouts/strongpoints were obliterated, resulting instantaneously in numerous casualties.

Back in the British positions, one private, knowing that this vast explosion was imminent, braced himself against the side of his trench with one leg pressed to the other side. The shock waves caused by the explosion were so intense that his leg was fractured below the knee.

Although almost certainly an apocryphal story, it was said that the explosion could be heard in Westminster, which gives some indication of the ferocity of the roar.

Those British soldiers who had edged out into No Mans Land, hoping to gain a crucial head start in the race to the enemy lines, were covered in the falling debris. But when they dusted themselves down and could once again open their eyes, what they saw was a very different vista; the gleaming white chalk set free from the bowels of the earth shone bright like some demented prize, drawing one towards it.

Beating the Germans in the foot race, soldiers of the Grimsby Chums got to the crater first. Here they set up on the lip of the crater nearest the Germans. Other men, some wounded, others lost, started to drip into the crater and joined the Chums. Then, finally, reacting to the blitz of war they had endured since 0730, the Germans began to recover and trained their fire onto those soldiers in the crater.

The plan had always been for soldiers of Major General Ingouville-Williams' 34th Division to attack and capture La Boisselle itself.

At zero hour, 3,000 men of the Tyneside Irish and Tyneside Scottish left the Tara-Usna Line and headed for La Boisselle with the order to advance beyond the positions currently held, secure the German trench systems and keep going.

However, if you look out from the crater to the Tara-Usna position, the problems immediately stack up. The Tyneside Irish had to cover almost one mile, in the open, before they even got to what had been the British jumping off position. Very few of these men made it. German machine guns, firing from their positions half a mile or so to the left of this crater, could sweep bullets across Sausage Valley and Avoca Valley further behind it. This was the route the Tyneside Irish had to take. After twenty minutes they had reached the jumping off trench. Without pause they then continued on through No

Avoca Valley.

Man's Land and into the German trench system. It was at this stage that many of those who had made it this far must have looked at one another and appreciated the reality of their situation. From an original force of 3,000 now only fifty men were still continuing; the rest were back where they started or cut down, killed or injured, by German fire.

Still the Geordies kept on; the remaining few fought their way through the trenches and set off for Contalmaison, a kilometre away. They advanced further than any other units had managed on that day, somehow managing to make it to Contalmaison, but the final assault was too much. The few dozen men could be no match for the German fortified village. This was the end of their heroic assault; this was where those brave men died.

Back here, at the crater itself, as the day developed, it became a magnet for artillery fire from both sides, until the British guns finally got the message that the crater was actually in British possession, and there it remained.

It is certainly the case that during this war, great heroism, inspirational deeds and great numbers of men died for meagre amounts of captured land.

It is also important to remember that this crater is a graveyard, as well as a memorial. There will be many Germans buried here.

Activities

Walk around the crater's edge, but do not attempt to climb down it – this is forbidden. The crater sides would have been much steeper and the bottom deeper but all have 'settled' over time. This is also a good opportunity to understand the depth of a front line system; look east to the top of the ridge running out to the south from the village – the main trench line of the German front line system was there.

5a. Fricourt German Military Cemetery

20 minutes

Return to the D20 in La Boisselle and turn right to Contalmaison. In the village turn right on the D147. Shortly after the sign for Fricourt the cemetery is on your left (signposted), with parking for a coach on the right.

Context

The only German cemetery on the Somme.

Orientation

During the war, this position was behind the German front lines of 1 July.

Spiel

In 1920 the French authorities began to construct this graveyard for burial of the bodies of German soldiers. In 1929, the German War Graves Agency (VKD) was allowed to take over the landscaping and care of this land. However, on the outbreak of the Second World War, work was suspended and did not begin again until 1966.

There are 17,027 soldiers buried here. They are soldiers from across the four years of war. It is important to remember just how few German bodies were actually saved from the battlefields for burial. It is difficult to be entirely accurate, but it is thought that as few as 10-15% are buried. The rest were returned home for burial, cremated or, to a much

Lines of German headstones – Fricourt.

larger extent, lay buried somewhere beneath the soil of the Western Front, entombed forever in the ground upon which they fell or in long lost cemeteries.

At Fricourt, only 5,057 men have identified graves, many of which are double burials. 11,970 men are buried in the four communal graves at the rear of the cemetery.

An interesting point to note, given what would occur after the war in which these men died, is the Jewish headstones. You will notice stones placed upon them; this is a sign of respect and remembrance and is supposed to represent the soil of Israel. You do not have to be a member of the Jewish faith to place a stone.

The famous fighter pilot ace Manfred von Richtofen, the Red Baron, was buried here in the early 1920s, being moved from the small cemetery where he was originally buried in 1918. He is still one of the most famous fighter pilots of all time, with an official figure of eighty combat victories. In 1925 his body was removed and sent to Berlin for reburial alongside past German war heroes and leaders. The Nazi regime would make much of his gravesite and importance as a true German warrior. This much travelled man, in life and death, was finally moved after the Second World War to a family plot, where he now rests at peace.

The village of Fricourt itself was in German possession before 1 July. It was superbly fortified and, when captured, it became a much reported example in the press back in Britain of how the Germans had prepared their defences and dug outs. The cellars of obliterated buildings had been incorporated into the trench systems and they were so well prepared that Tommies discovering them for the first time were stunned to see electric lighting, panelled walls, bunk beds, air shafts and even signs of female visitors; these were certainly different conditions to those to which they were accustomed.

Activities

Walk the cemetery. Talk to the group about the 'feel' of the place. Why are so few graves identified? Why is the cemetery so different to a British one? The mass graves are

A German Jewish headstone.

'... the Devonshires hold it still.'

concentrations generally from original German cemeteries elsewhere. Burial details were lost – or ignored – at the time of their concentration.

6. Devonshire CWGC Cemetery

15 minutes

Continue through the village to a major crossroads: turn left onto the D938 (towards Péronne); signs for the cemetery after 2km, which is off a narrow road. There is parking for a coach on a slip road opposite the cemetery.

Context

A particularly moving part of the Somme battlefield.

Orientation

Before you follow the track up and round to the cemetery, stand in the area where you have just disembarked your transport. Stand with your back to the copse (Mansell Copse) and look out past the D938 and into the fields. Looking slight left, at about 1030 on a clock face, you should just be able

Captain Duncan Martin.

to see the graveyard in front of the village of Mametz. In front of this was the position of The Shrine, which is important to the story of the Devonshires. So, therefore, you are stood in British front line territory, looking out across No Man's Land.

Spiel

Locate the gravestone of Captain Duncan L. Martin (A.1)

On 1 July, men of the 8/ and 9/Devons left their trench and made their way toward Mametz. This cemetery marks part of that front line. There are 163 men buried here. These men were those who left their trench and died in what are now the fields in front of the main road outside the cemetery. On the evening of 1 July their bodies were collected and brought back here for burial. They are, in effect, buried in the trench from which they attacked.

One man, Captain Duncan Martin, had anticipated what would happen to the men on that day. Whilst on leave he made a plasticine model of the ground they had to cross and the German positions in front. One point in particular was troubling him: The Shrine – a German machine gun position on the outside of Mametz village. His scale model proved his worries were not unfounded. It clearly showed that the 400 yards of land which the Devonshires had to cross were in open sight of the enfilade fire of the gun. They did not have a chance if it were not first destroyed. Martin passed on his concerns and, although a sympathetic response was received, no changes to the plan were made.

Captain Martin knew he would die. He is buried here alongside his men.

Outside the entrance to this cemetery is a stone memorial which includes these words: 'The Devonshires held this trench, the Devonshires hold it still.'

Activity

Walk the cemetery. Point out the position of The Shrine either before entering or after leaving (it is not visible from inside the cemetery itself).

7. Delville Wood/ South African National Memorial

45 minutes to 1.5 hours

Return to the D938, turning right, your original direction. After 4.2km, turn right onto the D197, towards Longueval, 5.6km. You will pass the point where the British and French lines met (marked by flagpoles). In Longueval, turn right at the crossroads on the D20 and in 400m turn left by the civil cemetery: signposted for the Memorial. Park in the car park, found a short distance on the left.

Context

South African Memorial, and a tranquil and reflective end to the day.

Orientation

On 1 July this area was deep inside German territory. The British front line was approximately 2.5 miles, south west from here, taking the reference point as the entrance to the memorial, opposite Delville Wood CWGC Cemetery.

Spiel

This is Delville Wood, site of the South African National Memorial.

That South Africa fought alongside the Allies in the war was controversial in itself, coming only twelve years since British forces triumphed over the Boer republics and the subsequent creation of the Union of South Africa as a Dominion of the Empire. Indeed, such was the intensity of feeling that the Prime Minister, General Louis Botha, first had to put down an Afrikaner rebellion against his decision before he could engage in the global conflict. The South African forces played a major role in the south African theatre of war, defeating German forces in German South West Africa (modern day Namibia), but many thousands also served on the Western Front.

The Memorial was dedicated in 1926 and commemorates more than 12,000 South African men who died during the Great War as well as a memorial to those who fought in the Second World War.

Delville Wood was deep inside German held territory in 1916. The British front line was approximately 2.5 miles south west from here. The men who fought for this land called it Devil's Wood, for very good reason.

Delville Wood lies on a section of high ground in the Somme battlefield area. During the 1916 offensive it was thought vital to capture this feature if British forces were going to be able to continue toward the German third line of defences. After the 9th (Scottish) Division suffered significant losses in their attacks on the village of Longueval, the attack on the wood was given to its reserve, the South African Brigade, which had been held back from the attack up to that point.

After launching this attack in the early hours of 15 July and capturing nearly all their objectives by midday, the South African Infantry Brigade underwent five days of the most brutal warfare imaginable; at one point it is estimated that shells were falling at 400 per minute on the hapless souls trying to hold the wood. The Germans threw nine of their very best available battalions into the mix, but still the South Africans held until, on 20 July, they were relieved. Of the 121 officers and 3,032 men who went into Delville Wood only 29 and 751 answered the roll call that day; fewer than 200 of those were in a fit state to fight any longer. What had been dense woodland was decimated, as was the South African Infantry Brigade.

The wood was not finally captured until just before 15 September, the opening of the third stage of the Somme offensive.

It is a poignant and reflective place where the scars of war remain but the beauty of life has fully returned. It is a fitting end to a day on the Somme.

Activities

Walking the re-grown wood itself; there is much to see. Stone markers carry the names given by the men to the rides in the wood which were designed for hunting; they are much wider today than they then were. You can clearly make out trench positions and much of the land is still shell marked. There remains one original tree from before the war. The memorial itself deserves close inspection and a good museum with restrooms and basic refreshment facilities are also located here.

The French Cemetery in Serre.

Additional Somme Visits

Below are ideas for extra visits to add to your tour if you are looking to extend it by up to another full day. I have given a brief description and an idea of where they would naturally fit, geographically, on the previous two days.

French Cemetery, Serre – after 1.

A recently restored and now very well maintained cemetery, containing 834 burials. Unusually, it was originally built and maintained by the CWGC until just prior to the Second World War.

Auchonvillers 'Ocean Villas' Tea Room – after 1a.

A great tea room run by Mrs Avril Williams, adjacent to an excavated trench. The cellar of the house tea room / restaurant was a first aid post during the Somme offensive. Packed lunches can be pre-ordered.

Poziéres Memorial to the Missing – after 4a.

This village was the scene of fierce fighting due to its location on the Albert-Bapaume road. By August the village was erased. The area, in general, is a location of much importance to Australian history and memorials to their actions can be found nearby. The memorial commemorates the missing from March to August 1918 on the Somme – those lost in the German offensive of this time.

Albert Town – after 5.

Not an easy stop for large groups to make, but a good stop if possible. It was here that on 15 January 1915 the golden virgin and child on the belfry of the basilica were hit by a shell, knocking them sideways but, crucially, not to the ground. Hence the legend grew that if the statue fell, the war would be over. This is a good R+R stop and there is a good museum to visit too.

Fricourt New Military CWGC Cemetery – after 5a.

133 graves of those from Yorkshire regiments who died on 1 July. The Tambour mine craters, blown under German positions as part of the first day offensive, can be seen beyond the Cross of Sacrifice.

38th (Welsh) Divisional Memorial – after 5a.

A striking red dragon which marks the spot where the Welshmen set off to fight through Mametz Wood itself, in which direction the dragon faces. From 7-12 July they suffered 4,000 casualties.

The impressive red dragon; the 38th (Welsh) Divisional Memorial.

New Zealand Memorial to the Missing, Caterpillar Valley CWGC Cemetery – after 6.

A memorial to 1,205 New Zealanders who have no known grave; also an excellent spot for observing the 'Battle for the Woods' – the series of German strong holds on high ground. Looking straight out from the entrance gates you will see High Wood in front, Bazentin to the left and Delville to the right. Straight ahead you will also be able to locate the obelisk of the New Zealand Memorial at Crest Farm. If you walk to the back of the cemetery, you can see Bernafay Wood with Trones Wood to its left.

* * *

Footnotes:

1. These timings are a rough guide and do not include any travel time between stops.
2. Serre was to be the hinge on which the push northwards swung. Those troops attacking further south of Serre would either hold or continue on deep into German-held territory.
3. However, the German machine gun prowess should not be overstated. In this section of the line the Germans actually had relatively few machine guns. Machine guns were best as enfilade weapon; that is they were designed to cover large areas predominantly from the side. What this highlights then is just how poor the British situation was if such German defences could cause so much damage.
4. Although not technically in the Somme region, but for the historical purpose I count it as so.
5. Billy McFadzean was awarded the Victoria Cross for his act of selfless heroism. His body was lost, perhaps obliterated during the shelling of that day, and so he is commemorated on the Thiepval Memorial, Pier and Face 15 A and 15 B.
6. Much of my account is based on the work of Martin Middlebrook. I cannot recommend his book on the Somme enough. He and his wife have also published an excellent battlefield guide to the Somme, *The Middlebrook Guide to the Somme Battlefields,* Pen & Sword Books, 2007.

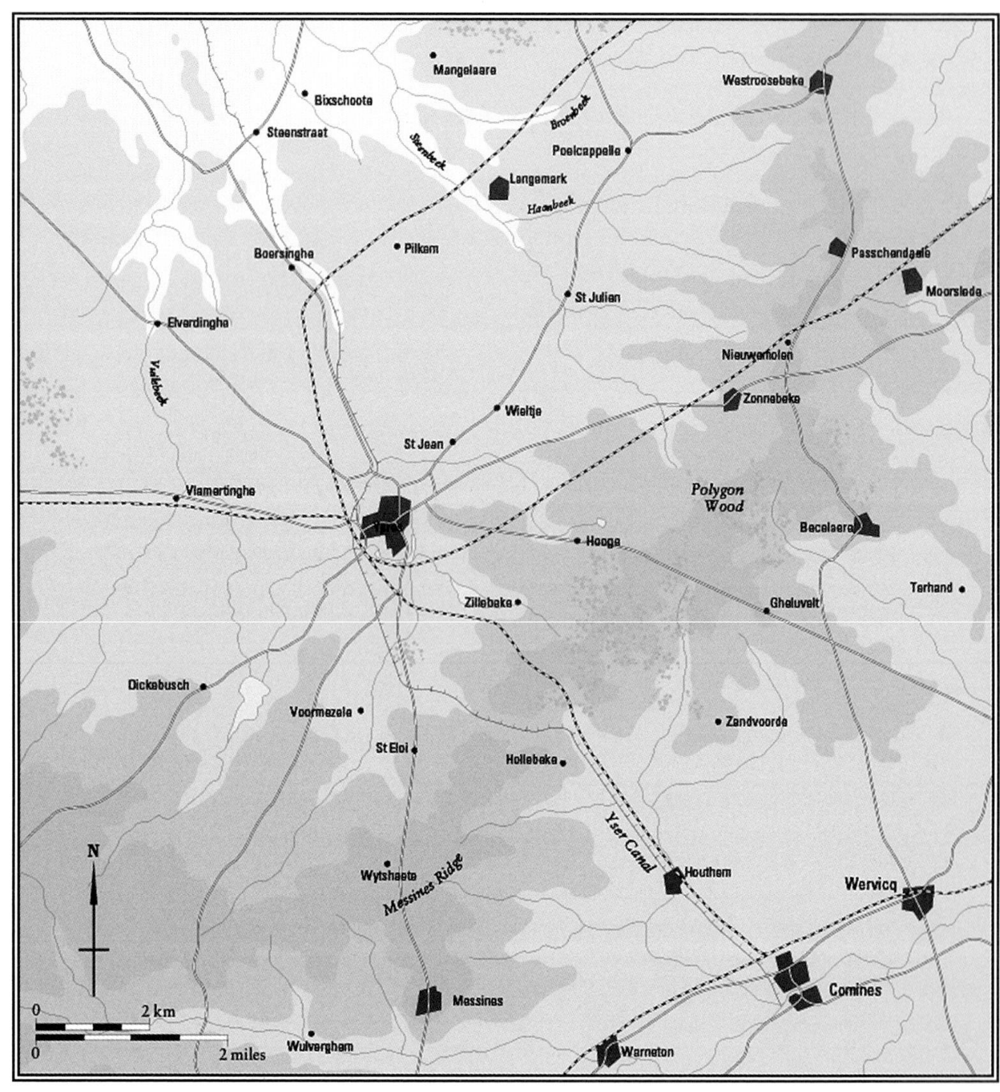

Map of the Ypres area.

Tour Two:

Ypres

Ypres is a town whose hold on me is relentless. Winston Churchill, speaking after the end of the war, said that 'a more sacred place for the British race does not exist in the world'. It is a place whose very presence keeps the war alive. It is truly possible to live history in all its raw and emotive parts here. Churchill wanted Ypres to be left obliterated, as it was in 1918, as a monument to the sacrifice of the British Empire. In this hope, I am delighted that his wishes did not come to pass. Ypres, today, is a beautiful city and one which remembers the sacrifices made in its defence. The vast majority of British troops who served on the Western Front during the war spent at least some time here; your visit is a pilgrimage in every sense of the word.

A brief pre-war history

Ypres is an ancient place. Raided by the Romans in the first century BC, its prosperity and importance was established during the Middle Ages. It was during the twelfth and thirteenth centuries that Ypres' main trading product, cloth, brought wealth to the area and gave reason for the drapers to build a magnificent and imposing Cloth Hall to act as the heart of the mini trading empire. The hall today is, like the whole centre of the town, rebuilt from the ashes of 1914-1918; but more of that later. It was also during this period that black cats were thrown from the top of the Cloth Hall in an act meant to purify and protect the city and its inhabitants from evil and witchcraft. Every three years Ypres remembers and resurrects this part of its history with the *Kattenstoet* (Festival of the Cats). You will be relieved to hear that real cats have now been replaced by the stuffed-toy variety. Be warned, I was there for the 2012 celebrations and, forgetting the overall odd nature of the event, it is the incessant cat noises looped through a speaker system in the Grote Market (the impressive central square) which will have you running for cover.

From the fourteenth century onwards, Ypres found itself besieged, conquered, hit by plague and ruinously managed. During the Hundred Years' War it was attacked by the Bishop of Norwich for three months, resulting in the usual starvation and desolation for the inhabitants in such circumstances. Plague hit in the fifteenth century and by the late sixteenth century the cloth trade was virtually dead. From a thirteenth century population of 40,000 the city now had a mere 5,000.

From the seventeenth century onwards, Ypres became a focus for political ambition and military strategy in realising it. The Spanish were ousted by 6,000 of Oliver Cromwell's troops in a pact with the French who then occupied the city, famously fortifying it through the work of the leading engineer of the time, Vauban. The Austrian-

Netherlands were rulers in the early eighteenth century before the French regained control just before that century ended.

Vauban's fortifications made this a potentially vital strategic location. Napoleon visited and inspected the city in 1804 and the British improved the fortification system further on their way to Waterloo in 1815.[1]

Very little of Vauban's fortifications survived into the twentieth century and Ypres, now very much a part of the newly established Belgium, was a relatively sleepy and forgotten part of Europe. That was, of course, until 1914.

Ypres during the Great War

Ypres' significance during the outbreak of the war was that it stood in the path of the planned invasion route of the sweep through Belgium and into France which the Schlieffen Plan dictated. After British troops first clashed with the Germans at Mons, they retreated to the Marne and Le Cateau, ultimately succeeding in halting the German army advance. Then followed the "race to the sea". What became known as the Immortal Salient was formed after the first Battle of Ypres in 1914 (see below) – an arc of defensive lines running eastwards from Boesinghe and then south, to just in front of Ploegsteert, with the town of Ypres positioned in the middle. Ypres, as the base of the bulge in the line, was a crucial part of the British supply line to the front; but it was also hugely vulnerable as it could be fired on from three (in fact, at some stages, four) sides. Hence, it was tactically vital to the British but at some point it took on something much more; it became symbolic of Allied efforts to hold back the German advance and thus took on a strategic quality. Ypres must not fall.

Ypres was under near constant shelling throughout the war but there were four major battles:

First Ypres: 19 October – 22 November 1914

This first battle was part of the closing stages of the "race to the sea". The British were desperate to protect the Channel ports and keep open their supply lines; the Germans, knowing that they must not be outflanked, still endeavoured to break through the British line in the hope of fulfilling their pre war plans. This would be the last signs of mobile warfare on the Western Front for over three years.

Initially, the British and French had pushed the Germans away from the city and on to the ridges which surrounded Ypres. From this position the Germans carried out several assaults on the British line. It was during this stage of the battle that the story of the "slaughter of the innocents" – enthusiastic patriotic German students who lost their lives in extreme numbers – was perpetuated and would go on to hold a significant place in Nazi propaganda as part of the "stab in the back" myth. When you visit Langemarck cemetery, these stories will be explored further.

At the end of October, the Germans did almost break the British line but, due to German command overestimating the size of the Allied forces in the area, they failed to exploit the success. By mid-November the fighting had, to a large degree, ceased. The war of movement was over. The British and French had held Ypres.

The battle had highlighted the problems which would dog fighting on the Western

Front for the following years. Holding a position was much easier than taking it. Also, German intelligence gathering and communication had been dire and were major contributions in preventing their victory. Overcoming these issues in a war with modern weaponry but poor and vulnerable lines of command and communication would bedevil both sides.

Second Ypres: 21 April – 25 May 1915

The German objectives were to capture Pilckem Ridge and other surrounding areas; in this they were largely successful due to the impact of the use of poison gas on a large scale on the Western Front for the first time. During the attack on Gravenstafel on 22 April, 6,000 French and colonial troops were incapacitated within ten minutes due to the release of Chlorine gas, with many Canadians also killed or injured later that same day by this psychologically terrifying weapon.

By 25 May Germany had carried out her last assault (another attack preceded with the release of gas) of the short campaign. Germany now held all the high ground surrounding Ypres and the Salient was fully formed. The rest of the war in this region could be best summarised as the Allies trying to remove the Germans from the ridges of high ground whilst the Germans settled in to position and shelled the British below.

It was after Second Ypres that Germany, perhaps in an act of spoilt-child petulance or, more fairly, in order to destroy the communication link, ramped up the artillery bombardment of Ypres. The city would be systematically destroyed. All civilians were now evacuated; they would return to rubble, dust and bones.

Third Ypres: 7 June – 10 November 1917

In spring 1917, the Allies had launched a co-ordinated offensive as part of Robert Nivelle's, the new French Commander-in-Chief, plan to break through the German fortifications above the River Aisne. The British advanced at the River Scarpe to limited success whilst the Canadians enjoyed triumph with the capture of Vimy Ridge, north of Arras, between 9-12 April and the 9th (Scottish) Division advanced even more significantly to the east of Arras on the 9th. The Battle of Arras was a diversion for the main thrust of the Nivelle Offensive. The French operations were disastrous. No breakthrough was achieved and with 187,000 casualties the morale of the army broke and mutinies spread. These mutinies largely took the form of a refusal to engage in any further offensive operations, rather than any out and out revolutionary fervour.

It was this that would lead to pressure on the British to maintain the operations on German positions on the Western Front so that General Pétain, replacing the disgraced Nivelle, could rebuild the shattered French armies. Essentially, the French needed time.

Field Marshal Sir Douglas Haig had long wanted to attack in Flanders; this had been his preference in 1916 but events at Verdun then forced his hand to attack on the Somme instead. His aim was to break through to the Belgian coast line, capture the ports, thus neutralising the very serious U-boat menace and disrupting German railway movement, before wheeling south to roll up the German line and achieve overall victory.

Messines 7-14 June 1917

In a rarity for this war, meticulous planning and preparation with genuine foresight and strategic thinking for an attack in the Messines Ridge area had been underway. The aim was to remove the German artillery's capacity to disrupt the forthcoming Third Ypres assault by enfilade fire from the high ground to the south. For over a year, tunnelling had occurred under the German strongpoints on the ridge. Shafts were dug to depths of a hundred feet and more and ammonal explosives painstakingly dragged through the claustrophobia-inducing cavities by very brave men working in perilously dangerous conditions. Eventually, one million pounds of explosives were laid in twenty-five mines. General Sir Herbert Plumer's Second Army was to carry out this assault.

On 7 June the charges were blown.[2] The explosion was so huge that the German garrison at Lille thought they were under attack and some people in England believed an earthquake was occurring. Although almost certainly an exaggeration, one estimate suggests that approximately 10,000 German soldiers were obliterated – some buried alive, others simply vanished – in that moment of earth-shattering intensity. The following attack was a complete success. The Germans - bewildered, stunned, beaten – simply struggled to operate. The Second Army took nearly all of its objectives on the first day. The element of surprise, combined with limited and achievable objectives, had proven to be a great success.

Third Ypres/Passchendaele 31 July – 10 November 1917

Unfortunately, Plumer would not be given, nor was it ever the intention to give him, the opportunity to follow up this initial success. Haig wanted to strengthen and prepare before making the main assault, to break out of the Salient to the east. He also placed the thrusting cavalryman, Sir Hubert Gough, in charge of this next part of the campaign; favouring his "breakthrough" potential over the "bite and hold" tactics of Plumer.

What this meant was that, as men and resources flooded the area in preparation for the attack, the German Army had six weeks to observe the movements and build up of the British.

Proceeding a ten-day artillery bombardment of the German positions (3,000 guns firing 4.25 million shells), troops left their trenches on 31 July. Though the first day went quite well, what followed was the imagery that many associate with the whole of the war. Flanders experienced the heaviest rainfall it had had for seventy years. The heavy shelling destroyed the complex and delicate drainage system of ditches and streams so that the whole vista became one long, continuous stretch of glutinous mud. This would be just as much an enemy to the advancing soldiers as any weaponry they faced. The soil in and around Ypres is largely made up of blue clay, which means that drainage is poor at the best of times. You do not need to dig deep to come across water. When you visit the trench systems at Sanctuary Wood you will likely see this for yourself.

Through the rain and mud, the offensive gained little success in early August and dragged on through the rest of the month before Haig called a temporary halt to operations, due to the appalling conditions. Plumer was then drafted back in to take on the next stage of the offensive. Making optimal use of a very dry September and staged "bite-and-hold"[3] tactics, Plumer enjoyed success at the Menin Road Ridge, Polygon Wood and Broodseinde. Then the appalling weather returned.

The final phase of the battle saw a month long campaign by Gough's Army and the French culminating, finally, in the capture of Passchendaele by Canadian forces on 6 November. This final stage of fighting had been horrific. The capture of the high ground on which the village stood gave Haig an excuse to call an end to the battle.

Casualty figures for this battle are disputed. If we take a middle estimate then both sides suffered around 300,000 casualties.[4] These are, clearly, brutal numbers. Historians continue to argue passionately about the necessity and legacy of this particular engagement. British Prime Minister Lloyd-George was famously scathing of Haig's conduct of this campaign in his memoirs but, of course, this was very much a part of the defence of his own legacy. The campaign had succeeded in removing the pressure from the French Army and it had inflicted a scale of casualties on the Germans with which they simply could not continue.[5] With the British also finding some success with the bite and hold tactics – which could be carried out across the Western Front on a limited basis, thus drawing German troops into combat across large areas of land at an increasingly constant rate – it can be argued that, for all the horrors of Third Ypres, the campaign forced the Germans to gamble in 1918 and thus laid the ground for Allied victory.

It is these controversies and considerations that, perhaps, will roll around in your mind as you make your journey across the land so viciously contested in 1917.

Fourth Ypres: 7-29 April 1918

Operation Michael (or the Kaiser's Offensive) opened on 21 March 1918. This was Germany's final attempt to try to win the war before arriving US forces provided an unstoppable number of troops for the Allied cause.

7 April was the beginning of an offensive by German forces to drive up through Neuve Chapelle and across the River Lys, heading north west to the channel ports. Initially this attack was a great success as the Germans recaptured the Messines Ridge and were close to splitting the Allied line, thus leaving Ypres open for encirclement. It was a very close run thing. Haig issued his famous 'backs to the wall' Order of the Day, which urged every man to fight to the last in the face of such an onslaught.

With a combination of Allied tactical withdrawal and German breakthroughs, the Allies gave up all the ground that they had fought so bloodily to capture in 1917. Ypres was on the brink. Yet the Germans, despite their seeming proximity to victory at this stage, were a nearly spent force. Ludendorff's advances had been impressive but the casualties were very heavy; he was now outrunning his supply lines and the soldiers were desperately tired. By the end of April, the battle at Ypres petered out. By August, the German army was exhausted and from then onwards the momentum laid with the Allies, whose "hundred days" drive to victory followed.

Finally, the front lines left Ypres.[6] The town, or what was left of it, as both a place of strategic necessity and symbolic importance, had survived.

After the war

In 1919 Ypres was a wasteland; a memorial to the sin of war. Yet work on recovering a future for the city from the death and destruction got under way almost immediately. Chinese labourers, Allied forces, German prisoners of war and the returning local population began the awful task of clearing and making safe the battlefields.

Ad hoc graveyards were everywhere, literally marking the places where men had fallen. Large cemeteries were left where they had sprung but many smaller ones were removed and bodies transferred to larger burial grounds. As the cemeteries were constructed and developed, the process to memorialise and remember also began immediately and by 1921 plans for the design of the Menin Gate were being considered.

Defying any early calls to leave the desolate city as a monument in itself, it was the returning civilian population who drove the rebuilding agenda. Why had the war been fought if not to secure their future?

Money from German reparations helped the resurrection; by 1925 the church (St Martin's Cathedral – although not actually a cathedral since 1801) was rising from the ashes and the main square also reborn. In 1934, work on rebuilding the Cloth Hall also began. All of this work was undertaken by following the original medieval plans.[7] The wretchedness of war would not be allowed to be the victor; hope would prevail.

Although under occupation during the Second World War, Ypres largely avoided further heartbreak during that conflict.

Battlefield tourism began almost immediately after the war. The first visitors were soldiers interested in revisiting where they had fought or travelling to visit the grave of comrades. In this last respect, many mothers and wives would make pilgrimages to the graves of their sons and husbands. In the years following the Second World War, interest in the First World War dropped off and so did visitors to Ypres but a resurgence of interest, driven by the dwindling numbers of veterans and then by significant anniversaries of events in the war, has seen the number of visitors increase exponentially. Visits by British school children, in particular, have helped drive the increase in visitors since the 1980s and help to keep the memory of the conflict alive.

As I said at the start of this short overview, Ypres is a truly wonderful place today. A visit to the city and its battlefields is an experience which makes an indelible imprint on one's soul.

In the following pages I outline a suggested series of visits for your itinerary, at the end of which I hope that you (and your students) will agree with me that a visit to Ypres is an affecting, emotional and truly life-changing experience.

* * *

The magnificent Ypres Cloth Hall.

Day One Itinerary

Approximate start time of 0900 and end time of 2015 (following the ceremony at the Menin Gate).

To get to all of these sites in one day is possible, but requires good pace. All those sites given a letter addition (i.e. 2a, 3b) are, although highly recommended visits, those stops that I would suggest better to leave out if time becomes an issue.

If you would rather take a more leisurely pace and prepare a lighter schedule, then you might only plan to visit the main stops (i.e. 1,2,3…) and if you find that you could do with adding another stop or two along the way, then bring in the lettered stop closest to your current location (i.e. if you have just visited 3 then go to 3a).

1. Sanctuary Wood CWGC Cemetery

2. Sanctuary Wood Trench System and Museum

2a. Front Line Hooge

2b. Lijssenthoek CWGC Cemetery and Visitor Centre

3. Poperinge

- Town
- Execution Post
- Talbot House

-LUNCH-

3a. Brandhoek New Military CWGC Cemetery

3b. Essex Farm CWGC Cemetery

3c. Yorkshire Trench

4. Langemark German Cemetery

5. Vancouver Corner

6. Tyne Cot CWGC Cemetery and visitor centre

-RETURN TO YPRES CENTRE-

-EVENING MEAL-

7. Menin Gate Ceremony

-DAY END-

Sanctuary Wood CWGC Cemetery.

1. Sanctuary Wood CWGC Cemetery

10-30 minute stop[8] - depending on whether this is your first day of the tour.

Take the N8 out of Ypres, heading east toward Menen (you are travelling on the infamous Menin Road). Straight across at the roundabout (this is Hellfire Corner, so called due to the incessant shelling of this area by the Germans, who were aiming to disrupt the British supply line to the front) and keep going approximately one kilometre further. Sanctuary Wood Museum will be signposted – take the exit to your right on to Canadalaan when it appears. Follow the road until you reach Sanctuary Wood Museum. Park at the museum and it is a short walk back to the cemetery that you will just have passed. The Canadian memorial beyond the museum has a turning circle for the coach.

Context

Many groups, particularly school groups, head straight for Sanctuary Wood Museum. This cemetery provides an ideal opportunity to set the scene for the day ahead and give calm and focus. This, in my experience, is crucial because of how busy the museum can be.

Orientation

Enter the cemetery and walk towards the Cross of Sacrifice. Go past this and you will come to an open area with some seating. Turn around and look back the way you walked. You are looking in the direction of the German front-line. This position (and the trench museum) were part of Sanctuary Wood. This is a good place to talk to your group.

Spiel

If this is the first stop on the first day of your tour:

- Give a short version of the overview history of the war (page 25)

For all tours:

- Give an overview of the importance of Ypres and the battles fought here (page 75)

Then:

This is Sanctuary Wood Cemetery. It is a concentration cemetery and did not exist during the war. In 1914 this was a wooded area and at the start of the war a quiet sector. However, toward the end of October, during the First Battle of Ypres, this relatively sleepy area was violently dragged from its slumber. The wood gained its name because it gave sanctuary to the British army as they treated their wounded during this battle and, as battalions were decimated, to regroup survivors into fighting units; the position was relatively safe and unshelled, whilst the trees gave some cover. However, by the end of November this was no more and the position became a magnet for artillery bombardment and infantry action for the rest of the war. In 1914, the German position to the east was over four kilometres away; in 1915 (after Second Ypres) it was less than two kilometres. During Third Ypres, it was much nearer to the front line positions. During Fourth Ypres, this position went behind the German front line. We will visit preserved sections of the Trenches momentarily.

If this is the first stop on the first day of your tour:

- Give an overview of the work of the Commonwealth War Graves Commission and explanation of the design and commemorations that the group will see.

Then:

This cemetery contains many burials from the First and Third Battles of Ypres.

There are 1,989 Commonwealth servicemen buried or commemorated in the cemetery. 1,353 of the burials are unidentified. Cemeteries had been started here in 1916, but were largely destroyed in 1917 and 1918. Hence, there are memorials at the rear of the cemetery for those soldiers known to be buried here but the exact location has been lost.

The most famous burial is that of Lieutenant Gilbert Talbot (I-G-1). It was as a memory of him Rev. P.B. 'Tubby' Clayton named Talbot House, a place for relaxation and religious observance, in Poperinge; you will visit it later today.

The one German burial is that of Hauptmann Hans Roser, Iron Cross holder and aviator.

Outside the cemetery is a private memorial to Lieutenant Keith Rae. After the war, his family had this memorial placed nearest to where he was last known to have been, near Hooge Crater. In order for its continued maintenance to occur, it was moved here in 1966.

A section of preserved trench at Sanctuary Wood.

Activity

If this is your first visit to a cemetery with the group, then five minutes to walk the rows whilst coming to terms with all the information they have just been given would be wise. Some will want to study the headstones, others simply contemplate.

Leave the cemetery. Turn right and walk back to the museum.

2. Sanctuary Wood Trench Museum

45 minutes to one hour

If booked in advance as a school group then approx. €6. As of the end of 2013 it is now €10 for an adult.[9]

Context

Without doubt, one of the most popular destinations for all battlefield tourists in the Ypres Salient. Jacques Schier, who sadly passed away in July 2014, was the famous custodian for many years. It was his grandfather who took the prescient decision to preserve this land as it was found at the end of the war. It still lives up to Rose Coombs' moniker as 'the only really authentic sector of trenches remaining in the salient'. There is an eccentric, but wonderfully so, museum which famously has old 1920s 3D photo viewers. The photos are unlike most that you or your students will have seen before; many are taken by the Germans and they are brutally uncensored – it is a good lesson for young minds to learn about the reality of what war actually does to the body of a man. There are also good examples of shell art and many original and unique artefacts are strewn outside as you enter the battleground area. The early German headstones are a particular favourite of mine.

Orientation

There is some disagreement amongst historians and battlefield guides as to exactly what part, and of which exact system, these trenches were. Some believe them to be part of a British second line from 1915/16 whereas others say that they are front line. It is quite possible that they are largely communication trenches. What is clear is that they are original (in situ and not reconstructed in entirety) and that it should not be a surprise that it is difficult to work out exactly their origin – remember that these trenches will have changed hands numerous times during the war, meaning that each side would have adapted them as the need arose.[10]

Spiel

Most students just want to explore the trench systems, bunkers and dug outs and get a feel for the place. This is probably the best way, but I would – with a pedant's hat on – urge you to try to stop youthful enthusiasm from turning into a full enactment of the war with hordes of groups running at each other making machine gun noises.

The visit does provide a useful opportunity to run through the basics of trench life:

Trenches developed in late 1914 when General Erich von Falkenhayn, after the German retreat to the River Aisne following the Battle of the Marne, ordered his men to dig continuous trenches that would provide them with protection from the advancing French and British troops. The Allies soon followed suit when it was clear that they could not break through the defences.

However, the crucial difference was that the Germans generally had been able to choose where they would stand, and then dig their trench systems there. That meant that

One of the most immediate and vivid visits in Ypres: Sanctuary Wood Trench Museum.

they, as you will see, seemed always to hold the highest ground and choose positions that were hidden from Allied sight. Many Allied soldiers, when capturing German positions, were shocked to discover the relative luxury that their enemy had been living in: concrete bunkers and even electricity were found.[11]

The British and French, therefore, had to live in much worse conditions. As you can see here at Sanctuary Wood, this often meant the low lying land, which in Ypres, because of its clay soil and poor drainage basin, means water when you dig.

Front line trenches were eight feet deep and six feet wide. The front of the trench was known as the parapet and the rear the parados. In front of the parapet would be placed sandbags (or earthen works) to absorb bullets and shrapnel. There would be a ledge to stand on so that the soldier could see over the top (the firestep). Trenches were not dug in a straight line but in ziz-zag or V patterns; this meant that if opposing soldiers stormed your trench, they could not just shoot all the way down and it also localised the damage from artillery blasts.

Duck boards were placed at the bottom of the trenches to protect soldiers from problems such as trench foot and also simply so that you could walk with some stability. Soldiers made small dugouts (funkholes) in the side of the trenches to give them some protection from the weather and enemy fire. In general, as previously mentioned, the German trenches were the most hygienic and comfortable to live in whilst the French ones were often awful. Private John Rea Laister paints a vivid picture upon recollection of visiting such a trench:

> 'We go down into thick slimy mud, it goes into your boots, creeps up your legs, goes around your privates, gets to about waist high. We're relieving the French, who were noted for burying their dead in the side of the trench instead of removing them […] all of a sudden an arm hits you in the face, buried in the side of the trench. You pass the word along, "Arm 'ere", you go a few more yards, you see a head hanging out, "Head 'ere".'[12]

An interesting point to consider is the philosophy and psychological constructs which the French army applied to trench warfare. Given pre war training for the offensive and also that their country had been invaded, it is easy to see why they rejected the idea of withdrawing to better ground and why they had no time for clean and ordered trenches; they did not want to sit still and they wanted Germany off their land. It is a point not to be underestimated when studying the French during the war.

Machine gun posts and barbed wire defences were deployed along the front line system and small observation trenches, or saps, were dug out into No Man's Land. These were used for listening posts, or for an advanced point to leave the trenches when on patrol.

Behind the front line trenches were support and reserve trenches, connected to the front line via communication trenches.

The trenches at Ypres were arguably at their most unpleasant during the first winter of the war. In this very cold 1914/15 period, the trenches were little more than shell holes with unrevetted,

The Salient is famous for its poor drainage due to the clay earth.

muddy and cramped dugouts. This is when most of the cases of trench foot occurred; it was largely unheard of after 1916.

Another point to note is that it took some time for both sides to master the art of trench warfare. Initially, the front line trenches were heavily manned as both sides adopted a 'hold ground at all costs' mentality. Yet this led to a drip-drip daily loss of men due to the relative ease for the enemy to drop mortars or shells into front line positions. The French often adopted a live-and-let-live policy in their sectors, whereas the British always rejected this and would seek to train some fire on enemy trenches daily.

The museum itself is unique and eclectic.

Eventually, the Germans, then the Allies, adopted a much more fluid and flexible system. In this development the front line was held by a minimal force with the strength in defence being held in support trenches. This shift in mentality limited losses in the front line whilst drawing the enemy in to an unfamiliar trench system, only to be forced back out by waves of defenders held further back.

The width of No Man's Land varied considerably; it might be as much as a thousand yards or, as at Vimy Ridge, just a matter of yards. The experience of the soldiers is also severely misunderstood by many. They simply did not spend all their time in the front line and they did not spend all their time fighting. Many veterans who survived the war would recall going over the top once or twice. The British army rotated its men constantly and a soldier would usually only spend ten days per month in a front line position. The rest would be spent in support positions or behind the lines; though these still held the dangers of enemy shelling and carrying up munitions and supplies to the men at the front. The real horror for many men was the combination of boredom and proximity to death; at any moment a shell might obliterate you and your comrades. It was that thought that most feared, not the fear of battle but the fear of instant nothingness.

What can be said with certainty is that the Ypres sector had some of the worst trench conditions throughout the war and was always under fire – it was not a place that most soldiers were pleased to be sent to. For large parts of the war, many other areas of the British line were relatively quiet in comparison unless, of course, a major action was in progress.

Activity

Explore the trenches! There are toilets and a café. The museum provides an opportunity to study and discuss the uniforms and evolution of helmets. There are some fabulous examples of trench art – who made these and why are other interesting conversations to be had.

2a. Front Line Hooge

20-30 minute

Entrance fee: donation; suggestion €1-2 per person

Head back to the N8, turn right and continue heading east on the Menin Road. You are heading for Hooge – scene of some of the heaviest fighting in the Salient. You will see Hooge crater cemetery on your right and to the left are Hooge crater itself, a museum and Hotel Kasteelhof't Hooghe a little further on. Park where possible and head for the hotel.

Context

An alternative to Sanctuary Wood Museum or an additional stop. Of main interest are the excavated trenches, concrete bunkers and crater in the grounds of the hotel.

Orientation

Standing at Front Line Hooge (any part of the site), look in the direction of the Menin Road heading further out of Ypres and you are looking in the direction of German positions at the end of 1914 (as explained below, this site would change hands throughout the war).

Spiel

Some of the heaviest fighting in the Salient took part in the grounds of the old Chateau at Hooge. Today, the theme park and hotel stand on the site of the original chateau and its stables. In 1914 it was the HQ of Major General Monro and was shelled for the first time on 31 October. Six officers were killed and the destruction of the chateau had begun.

On 19 July 1915, in what was then the largest ever use of ammonal explosive (at 3,500lbs, this would be dwarfed by the 60,000lbs blown at the Lochnagar Crater on the Somme in 1916), mines were blown by the British at Hooge. This crater then became an important tactical position that both sides would fight over for the rest of the war. The pond in the grounds of the hotel is not the crater left by that huge explosion, but it is certainly a crater left by the mine fighting of 1915-1916.

The first use of the flamethrower (*flammenwerfer*) by the Germans against the British took place here to great effect in the early hours of 30 July 1915, spreading panic amongst

Part of the 'iron harvest' on display at Hooge Crater.

Hooge Crater offers a good opportunity to explore a concrete bunker.

the British as twenty five yard jets of flame engulfed their positions. The British recaptured the crater by August but then suffered over 4,000 casualties in an attempted attack launched from here and close by in September.

By summer 1916, the Germans had recaptured all of Hooge following the blowing of several mines underneath Canadian positions. The British retook the area during Third Ypres in 1917, only to be driven out again during the Kaiser's Offensive in 1918.

On 28 September, the British captured Hooge for the final time as the Germans were pushed relentlessly out of Flanders.

Look around you; this small hotel, theme park and pond do not seem that remarkable today. The world moves on and people go about their everyday lives. But Hooge, as a microcosm of the sheer effort and loss endlessly displayed during the war, is the kind of place which can hit you straight between the eyes. For most of the war, this site was the front line; its history is astonishing.

Activities

You can walk the grounds of the Front Line Hooge area. Information boards explain some of the history and show where the trenches were. One trench has been excavated and it is possible to explore one of the concrete bunkers.

If you have time, there is an excellent and recently extended museum in the old chapel opposite the cemetery. A visit to the cemetery is, of course, worthwhile too.

2b. Lijssenthoek CWGC Cemetery and Visitor Centre

30 minutes

Head back toward Ypres on the N8.[13] When you get to Ypres, follow signs for the N308 towards Poperinge. When you reach Poperinge, head on the R33 Poperinge ring road. The R33 (Poperinge) continues to the left hand junction with the N38 Frans-Vlaanderenweg. 800 metres further along the N38 is a left hand turning onto Lenestraat. Take the next right on to Boescheepseweg. The cemetery is 2km along Boescheepseweg on the right hand side of the road. In late 2012, a new visitor centre was built which offers ample parking.

Context

A personal favourite of the author; there are a huge variety of burials on what is the site of several Casualty Clearing Stations (CCS). It is the second largest cemetery in area and offers an opportunity to discuss supply lines, medical treatment and women in the war. The excellent new visitor centre is also worth seeing; it both highlights the stories of some of those buried here whilst focusing on the medical history of the CCS. It is free to enter.

Orientation

At the back of the cemetery was the old railway line which took supplies to the front line and brought wounded men back to the CCS for treatment. Gather the group near the Stone of Remembrance.

Spiel

Lijssenthoek cemetery contains 10,784 burials; 7,332 are British with the rest being from a huge variety of nationalities. There are other Commonwealth nations, German, American and Chinese burials here. The reason for the huge variety is closely tied to the history of this location. The farm here was used by the French as an evacuation hospital in 1914, with the British establishing a Casualty Clearing Station in 1915 and the French using the site again in 1918.

Injured soldiers from the front lines, where we have been this morning, would be sent back behind the lines to receive medical treatment. A railway line, which ran at the back

of this cemetery, brought many of the men here. Given the nature of many of the injuries and the rudimentary medical treatment available, many men died and thus this cemetery was here right from 1914. It is notable that King George V visited Lijssenthoek during his 1922 Pilgrimage to the battlefields.

Walk back toward the entrance, but do not leave the cemetery; instead walk down the first row of graves – to your left as you look at the entrance from inside the cemetery. You are looking for the grave of Nellie Spindler (XVI–A–3). Gather around the headstone.

Among the 10,000 men in this cemetery lies one woman. This is the grave of Staff Nurse Nellie Spindler. She is one of only two British female First World War casualties buried in Belgium. She was from Wakefield in West Yorkshire. On 21 August 1917 she was working at a CCS in Brandhoek when it came under fire from German artillery. What happened to Nellie is described by the sister in charge of the CCS:

'Bits [of shells and debris] came over everywhere, pitching at one's feet as we

Lijssenthoek, its size and history are moving for all who visit.

> rushed to the scene of the action, and one just missed one of my Night Sisters getting into bed in our Compound. I knew by the crash where it must have gone and found Sister E. as white as paper but smiling happily and comforting the terrified patients. Bits tore through her Ward but hurt no one. Having to be thoroughly jovial to the patients on these occasions helps us considerably ourselves. Then I came on to the shell hole and the wrecked tents in the Sisters' Quarters at [CCS] 44. A group of stricken M.O.'s [medical officers] were standing about and in one tent the Sister was dying. The piece went through her from back to front near her heart. She was only conscious a few minutes and only lived 20 minutes. She was in bed asleep. The Sister who shared her tent had been sent down the day before because she couldn't stand the noise and the day and night conditions. The Sister who should have been in the tent which was nearest was out for a walk or she would have been blown to bits; everything in her tent was... It all made one feel sick.'[14]

The CCS moved to Lijssenthoek, where Nellie was buried, with full military honors and the Last Post was played.

Activities

Time to explore the cemetery. The Chinese graves are usually of particular interest; many of these men will have died from the 1918-1919 influenza 'Spanish flu' outbreak. They were employed to clear up the battlefields after the war. You may wish to go to the grave of Private William Baker (XXV-B-22) who was 'Shot at Dawn' as a prelude to the visit to the execution post at Poperinge later in the day. Also, there used to be many more American burials here – a discussion on repatriation differences between combat nations might be interesting; American servicemen and women who died on active duty are all eligible for burial at Arlington National Cemetery in Washington D.C. or at a private cemetery elsewhere in the U.S.A.[15]

Lijssenthoek contains burials from a range of nationalities spanning the years of the war.

3. Poperinge

1 – 2 hours

Reverse the route just travelled and head for Poperinge. Follow the signs for the centre. Once in the central square, there is space for a coach to drop off and pick up outside the church.

The Town …and Ginger!

With the Town Hall at your back, walk into the central square (Grote Markt). Keep walking down the street. You will pass a pharmacy on your left (one location of Skindles officers' café during the war) and on the opposite side of the road will be the Hotel Belfort. Keep walking until you come to La Poupée. Stop outside here.

Context

Poperinge's light side.

Spiel

Poperinge (spelt Poperinge in 1914) or 'Pop' was the epicentre for Tommy rest and recuperation for those in the Salient. It is eight miles to the west of Ypres and was largely (though not entirely!) out of the range of the German guns. Therefore, vital supplies were stored and/or travelled through here on the way to the front. More importantly, this was where soldiers heading out of the Salient could come to feel alive again.

It is estimated that at its height there were up to 250,000 allied personnel passing through here over a short period of time. The entrepreneurial spirit was at its height; young men, with money, not knowing what future they have, are always good customers given the right sort of enterprises. Thus, officers clubs, saloons, illicit gambling and prostitution (not illicit!) quickly established themselves.

One of the most infamous cafés was 'La Poupée'; its notoriety was built upon the attractions of a particular young lady. Writing in his diaries, Captain Edwin Campion Vaughan gives us a glimpse:

> 'Our next visit was to a café in the square – La Poupée. The two rooms were full of diners but we found a table in the glass-roofed garden. A sweet little sixteen-year-old girl came to serve us. I fell a victim at once to her long red hair and flashing smile. When I asked her her name, she replied 'Gingair' in such a glib way that we both gave a burst of laughter. We had a splendid dinner, with several bottles of bubbly, and Ginger hovered delightfully about us. Over our cigars and liqueurs I offered her my heart, which she gravely accepted.'[16]

We will hear more from Vaughan later. However, not all the men wanted such carnal pleasure.

Head down Gasthuisstraat (the road with Spar on it). Walk for five minutes and you will come to 'Toc H'/Talbot House.

Alas, Ginger is no longer there (although there is a photo of her inside).

Talbot House

www.talbothouse.be if you wish to arrange a visit inside. €5 per student on a school group visit. €8 for an individual adult. (Entrance to the museum is not on this street but take the next right and you will and it is about forty yards away, on your right.)

Context

Spiritual retreat. A visit inside will take at least one hour, hence the flexibility in suggested time for the stay in Poperinge. The house still offers accommodation and the Chapel is very special, given it is much as it was during the war. You can look around the house, gardens and watch a recorded re-enactment of a typical Tommies' concert.

Spiel

Even if you are not intending to go inside, it is worth telling your group, either outside Toc H or in the Grote Markt, about the place as an apt prelude to the last Pop visit.

On December 11 1915 Talbot House or, in army signallers' terms, Toc H, opened its doors. Reverend Neville Talbot had been searching for somewhere to house a church club when this property became available. He asked a friend, Reverend Philip Byard 'Tubby' Clayton to head up the project. The idea was for Toc H to be an oasis of calm, contemplation and respite for exhausted soldiers who, away from the base pleasures of the rest of the town (there would be no alcohol, and certainly no prostitution!), could read, talk, pray… be human again. No rank would be acknowledged, men and officers mixed freely. The house was named after Neville's brother, Gilbert, whose grave we visited at Sanctuary Wood this morning.

After the war the house was reclaimed by its former owner (who had rented it to Tubby) and Toc H had to close; that was until Lord Wakefield purchased the house in 1929 and its doors were opened once again. In 1919, Tubby had returned to London and from there he established the Toc H (Christian) Movement, whose purpose was to encourage people to 'think fairly, to love widely, to witness humbly and to build bravely'. This movement spread across the globe and still operates today.

So, we have seen Poperinge as both a place of debauchery and spiritual solace; now we shall see its darker side.

Walk back to the Grote Markt square. Head straight for the town hall/information centre and take the road to the immediate left of it. This is Guido Gezellestraat. After 20 seconds or so, you will come to a large archway on your right with double red doors. Go in![17]

Execution Post and Cells

Free Entry

Context

The dark side of Pop.

The cells are immediately to your right as you enter. The execution post is in the small courtyard.

Military executions remain one of the more controversial aspects of the war.

Spiel

During the First World War there were 346 Military executions of British and Commonwealth troops by their own forces. These executions were largely carried out on soldiers who had deserted their posts or, much less commonly, those who had displayed acts of cowardice; the aim was to discourage others from doing similar. One, Private James Crozier, was only 16 years old when he was 'shot at dawn'.[18]

On the evening before the execution, a chaplain would visit the condemned. In the morning, the man would sometimes be given copious amounts of rum and would then be led out to face a firing squad. Tied to a stake, blindfolded and with a piece of white cloth pinned over the man's heart, a prayer would be said. At least six soldiers would make up the squad; sometimes one would have a blank round, though he would, of cause, be aware from the recoil whether it was blank or live.

The officer would give the command. Shots would ring out. The attending medical officer would check that the man was dead; if he were still alive then the officer would shoot him with his revolver.

We have just taken a very short walk from Poperinge's good-time centre, yet we are a million miles away from that revelry now. Imagine, also, the psychological effect of the location of this post – a soldier enjoying a *vin blanc* may be only too aware of his proximity to this site.

This is a hugely controversial aspect of the war. Many of these men we would now recognise as suffering from Post-Traumatic Stress Disorder and in 2006 all were posthumously pardoned. Yet, to judge history by the standards of our own time is a dangerous approach. For the British army, with a huge volunteer and then conscript army in the field, maintaining discipline was vital; a look at events in Russia and at the French after the Nivelle Offensive highlight how possible revolution and mutiny were.

Still, we cannot get away from the thought of very scared young men having their lives taken, not by the enemy, but by their own side. Take some time to reflect.

Activities

Explore the cells.

Leave the cells and head back to the Grote Markt square.

This is often a good opportunity to give the group some free time to eat their packed lunches or for a quick stop at a café and a little explore.

3a. Brandhoek New Military CWGC Cemetery

10 minutes

Leave Poperinge by the N308 towards Ypres. As you head into the small hamlet of Brandhoek you will see a right turning onto Grote Branderstraat. The cemetery is signposted, but be aware that there are two others nearby.

Context

One of the most famous stories of personal bravery and a double Victoria Cross winner.

Orientation

After parking up, follow the signposts to the cemetery which is placed in a beautiful little spot behind some houses. You are looking for the grave of Captain Noel Chavasse VC and Bar, MC (Plot 3-B-XV); this is easily spotted by the abundance of poppy crosses laid before it. Gather around.

Spiel

The burials in this cemetery are of men who died during the Third Ypres campaign. This grave is that of Captain Noel Chavasse VC and Bar, MC, a doctor and officer in the Royal Army Medical Corps (RAMC). Chavasse was a first-class Oxford graduate and ran the 400m in the 1908 Olympic Games. In 1913 he joined the RAMC.

During the war, Chavasse was a captain attached to the 1/10th (Scottish) Battalion of the

Noel Chavasse, double VC.

King's (Liverpool) Regiment. He was awarded the Military Cross (third highest gallantry award) in 1915 and was Mentioned in Dispatches (name mentioned in the official report of an action or campaign – usually relating to bravery or exceptional performance of some kind).

However, as you will see from his headstone, he is most remembered for being one of only three people to ever win the Victoria Cross twice (highest award in the British and Commonwealth Armed Forces; awarded for valour "in the face of the enemy") and the only man in the First World War to have done so. The following two citations, published in *The London Gazette,* tell his story:

Relating to his actions on August 9th, 1916 at Guillemont on the Somme:

> 'Captain Noel Godfrey Chavasse, M.C., M.B., Royal Army Medical Corps.
>
> For most conspicuous bravery and devotion to duty.
>
> During an attack he tended the wounded in the open all day, under heavy fire, frequently in view of the enemy. During the ensuing night he searched for wounded on the ground in front of the enemy's lines for four hours.
>
> Next day he took one stretcher-bearer to the advanced trenches, and under heavy shell fire carried an urgent case for 500 yards into safety, being wounded in the side by a shell splinter during the journey. The same night he took up a party of twenty volunteers, rescued three wounded men from a shell hole twenty-five yards from the enemy's trench, buried the bodies of two Officers, and collected many identity discs, although fired on by bombs and machine guns.
>
> Altogether he saved the lives of some twenty badly wounded men, besides the ordinary cases which passed through his hands. His courage and self-sacrifice, were beyond praise.'

The following was his citation for his second award, earned between 31 July-2 August, 1917 north east of Ypres:

> 'His Majesty the KING has been graciously pleased to approve of the award of a Bar to the Victoria Cross to Capt. Noel Godfrey Chavasse, V.C., M.C., late R.A.M.C., attd. L'pool R.
>
> For most conspicuous bravery and devotion to duty when in action.
>
> Though severely wounded early in the action whilst carrying a wounded soldier to the Dressing Station, Capt. Chavasse refused to leave his post, and for two days not only continued to perform his duties, but in addition went out repeatedly under heavy fire to search for and attend to the wounded who were lying out.
>
> During these searches, although practically without food during this period, worn with fatigue and faint with his wound, he assisted to carry in a number of badly wounded men, over heavy and difficult ground. By his extraordinary energy and inspiring example, he was instrumental in rescuing many wounded who would have otherwise undoubtedly succumbed under the bad weather conditions.
>
> This devoted and gallant officer subsequently died of his wounds.'

Noel Chavasse, the most highly decorated soldier of the war; remembered because of his selfless acts of bravery in saving others with little regard for his own well being. Never has recognition been more deserved.

Return to your transport

3b. Essex Farm CWGC Cemetery

20 minutes

Join the N38. After 7 km take the exit toward Diksmuide. Turn left on to Diksmuidseweg and you will see the cemetery on your right.

Context

One of the most frequently visited cemeteries for visitors to the Western Front. It is the site that inspired John McCrae to write *In Flanders Fields* and contains other notable burials and bunkers. However, the abundance of visitors takes something away from the place, hence this being an additional rather than main visit.

Orientation

There is a McCrae Memorial stone with the full text of his poem outside the cemetery. To the left of the cemetery you will find Advanced Dressing Station (ADS) bunkers. At the back of the cemetery is the memorial obelisk to the 49th (West Riding) Division, who served along these canal bank sectors for the longest continuous period and have many men buried here.

Spiel

This can be delivered from any part of the cemetery – find a quiet spot, if possible.

This is Essex Farm Cemetery and, during the war, was the site of an Advanced Dressing Station where soldiers would be brought straight from the front-line to receive urgent medical treatment. The ADS was established in 1915 by the 4th Division but was then taken over by the Candian Army Medical Corps during Second Ypres. They treated many gas cases in the ADS, which we will soon visit. In 1915 these bunkers were little more than holes in the ground supported by wood and iron, but were strengthened into the concrete bunkers you see today in time for Third Ypres.

One of the Canadian officers serving here in 1915 was Captain John McCrae. On 2 May, one of McCrae's friends, Lieutenant Alexis Helmer, was eviscerated by a direct hit from an 8 inch shell. Helmer was buried and a wooden cross placed over his grave. Seeing the ever growing numbers of wooden crosses outside the ADS, McCrae was moved to write what has become the most famous poem of the war:

In Flanders fields the poppies blow
Between the crosses, row on row,

That mark our place; and in the sky
The larks, still bravely singing, fly

Scarce heard amid the guns below.
We are the Dead. Short days ago

Rifleman Valentine Joe Strudwick, who died at the age of 15.

We lived, felt dawn, saw sunset glow,
Loved and were loved, and now we lie

In Flanders fields.

Take up our quarrel with the foe:
To you from failing hands we throw

The torch; be yours to hold it high.
If ye break faith with us who die

We shall not sleep, though poppies grow

In Flanders fields.

In Flanders Fields was published in *Punch* magazine in December that year, and has become a symbol of the sacrifice of the war. Helmer's grave cannot be found in the cemetery; it was destroyed and lost by later fighting in the area. He is commemorated: Menin Gate (Panel 10).

You may wish to visit the grave of Rifleman Valentine Joe Strudwick (I-Z-8). You will be able to locate this relatively easily due to the number of crosses placed at it (and likely visitors stood around). Strudwick was only 15 years old.[19]

Activities

Visit the monuments and ADS bunkers. There are also further bunkers north of these which can be reached by continuing on beyond the ADS.

ADS Bunker, Essex Farm.

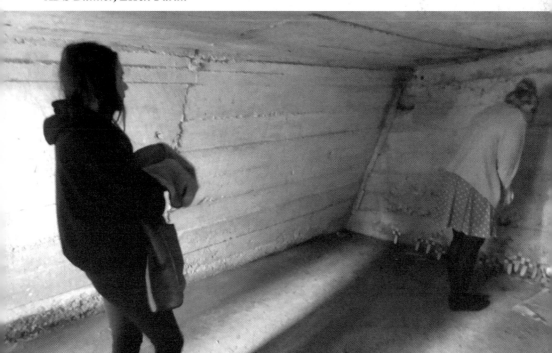

3c. Yorkshire Trench

Continue on the N369 until, after approximately 2km, you can cross over the canal on the Brugstraat. Keep right onto Molenstraat and then continue on to Langemarksewerg. After a few hundred metres turn right onto Bargiestraat (keep your eyes peeled for the small signs directing you to the Yorkshire Trench. Yes, it is in the middle of the industrial park! Keep following the road around and the trench will be found on your left.

10 minutes

Free entry

Context

A section of British trench from 1915/16, reconstructed and concrete sandbagged. An excellent photo opportunity stop, made all the more surreal by its position in the middle of an industrial park!

Orientation

Standing in the trench, you are in the British 1915/16 front-line position.

View from the Yorkshire Trench.

One of the more unusually sited spots on the Battlefield tour route: the Yorkshire Trench.

Spiel

A group of local amateur archaeologists, The Diggers, made the discovery of a 1917 British dugout and this 1915/16 trench position as they excavated the site whilst the foundations for the industrial park were being dug in 1992. They discovered a wealth of artefacts, ranging from uniforms to grenades and bullets, which were in superb condition due to preservation by the water and mud of the region. You will see many of these on display in the In Flanders' Fields Museum. They also discovered 155 remains of soldiers who had been interred by the mud for so long. Many of the British discovered here were from an action on 6 July 1915.

The Diggers have continued their work and found underground chambers, tunnels and trenches throughout the region. It is an unsettling thought to consider just what remnants of war lie a few feet below. Every footstep you take is on hallowed ground.

Activities

Trench walk through.

4. Langemark German Cemetery

50 minutes

Head north on the N369 (Diksmuidseweg) for 2km and then continue onto Randweg. Turn right, over the canal, on the Brugstraat and bear right and continue onto Langemarkseweg. Continue on to Langemark for approximately 4.5km. Turn left when you come to the junction with Zonnebekestraat. Head through Langemark on this road, which becomes Klerkenstraat. The road will take you out of the town and the cemetery is on your left.

Context

A deeply affecting visit to a German cemetery; certainly a part of the tour which stays with one for a long time. It is never pleasant, but always powerful.

Orientation

You will walk through a visitors' portal which contains audio and video content (already enough to alter the mood). As you head through the main entrance to the cemetery, take note of the entrance (you will reference it later), the main burial pit in front of you and the pill boxes to your right. However, head towards the back of the cemetery, somewhere near the bronze statues and gather.

Brooding, intense and memorable: Langemark German Cemetery.

Spiel

If you want to know the difference between winning and losing a war, then look around. This is Langemark German cemetery and it is one of the most affecting places in Flanders. It is sombre, brooding, dark; it feels a degree or two colder in here.

Remember back to the vast expanse of land that was Lijssenthoek [*if you have been*] – the beautifully kept, light and welcoming Commonwealth cemetery. There were 10,000 burials there. In that small rectangular space near the entrance to this cemetery is a burial pit. It is known as the *Kameraden Grab* (Comrades Grave). It contains the remains of 24,917 German soldiers.[20] The total number of burials here is 44,292. If grief describes anything then it describes the feeling of this place.

The burial of the German dead was, not surprisingly, a much more contentious issue than those of the victorious nations. In the immediate years after the war it was the British who handled this work before the Belgians took over. In 1925, during Germany's renaissance and acceptance back into the international community (the 'Golden Years'), a treaty was signed between Belgium and Germany which meant that in 1929 the Germans took over the care of the cemeteries. There were, initially, hundreds of cemeteries, but nearly all of them were eventually concentrated into four cemeteries in Belgium. When the Second World War broke out, work on these sites was, understandably, halted. Work was not actually finished here until the 1980s.

About 3,000 of the burials here are of the Student Volunteers who died in the battle of Langemark in October and November 1914 – a vitally important national story, especially important as a propaganda tool to Hitler and the Nazis; here were half-trained young patriots who died heading courageously into battle, to be slaughtered by machine gun fire, whilst singing 'Deutschland, Deutschland, über alles', or so the myth goes. In 1940, Hitler visited here. He stood by the pillboxes with hundreds of other Nazis, viewing this place and believing that he had overturned the legacy of that war and delivered a German

The truly shocking Kameraden Grab.

Reich that would last a thousand years. There is a photograph of him leaving here, out of the main entrance, under a corridor of Nazi salutes. This pageantry, fascism and national rebirth would be short lived but, for Hitler, Langemark was a reason for the Second World War; it linked the two in his mind and its importance cannot be underplayed. Under Hitler's reign as Führer, 11 November in Germany became 'Langemarck Day' as a counter to Armistice Day. However skewed, or factually incorrect, the "slaughter of the innocents" at Langemark left an imprint on Hitler's soul.

Earlier today, I read an extract from the diaries of Edwin Campion Vaughan, a captain in the Royal Warwickshire Regiment, with a fond eye for Ginger! His diaries are a brilliant insight into life in the Ypres Salient in 1917. The following extract is his description of an attack on 27 August during the Third Ypres campaign, during which his battalion is tasked with capturing Langemark Ridge. Vaughan led D Company. The action that follows occurred over the land two to three miles south-east of here *(with your back to the rear of the cemetery it is roughly to your right)*:

> 'An instant later, with one mighty crash, every gun spoke, dozens of machine guns burst into action and the barrage was laid. Instantaneously the enemy barrage crashed upon us, and even as I rose, signalling my men to advance, I realized that the Germans must have known of our attack and waited at their guns.
>
> 'Shells were pouring on to the St Julien-Triangle Road as we advanced, and through the clouds of smoke and fountains of water I saw ahead the lines of figures struggling forward through the mud [...] I saw, with a sinking heart, that the lines had wavered, broken, and almost disappeared.
>
> '[...] standing on the road in front with drums of ammunition in each hand, I saw Lynch shaking and helpless with fear. I ran out and told him to go forward. "Oh, I

Reading 'Vaughny'.

can't, Sir, I can't," he moaned. "Don't be a fool," I said, "you will be safer in the gunpits than you are here – right in the barrage." "Oh, I can't walk," he cried, and I shook him. "You know what your duty is," I told him. "Are you going to let Rogers and Osborne and the rest go forward while you stay here?" "No, Sir!" he said, and ran across the road. Before he had gone three yards he fell dead.

'[…] Immediately there came the crackle of bullets and mud was spattered about me as I ran, crawled and dived into shell holes, over bodies, sometimes up to the armpits in water, sometimes crawling on my face along a ridge of slimy mud around some crater […] I saw a head rise above a shell-hole, a mouth opened to call something to me, but the tin hat was sent flying and the face fell forward into the mud. Then another head came up and instantly was struck by a bullet. This time the fellow was only grazed and, relieved at receiving a blighty, he jumped out, shaking off a hand that tried to detain him. He ran back a few yards, then I saw him hit in the leg; he fell and started to crawl, but a third bullet got him and he lay still.

'[…] Up the road we staggered, shells bursting around us. A man stopped dead in front of me, and exasperated I cursed him and butted him with my knee. Very gently he said "I'm blind, Sir," and turned to show me his eyes and nose torn away by a piece of shell.

'[…] Around us were numerous dead, and in shell-holes where they had crawled to safety were wounded men […] they cheered us faintly as we passed.

'[…] I entered Springfield, which was to be my HQ. It was a strongly-built pillbox, almost undamaged.

'[…] On one of the machine gun niches lay an unconscious German officer, wearing two black and white medal ribbons; his left leg was torn away, the bone shattered and only a few shreds of flesh and muscle held it on. A tourniquet had been applied, but had slipped and the blood was pouring out […] I made him comfortable […] until at last he lay quiet.

'[…] Suddenly I heard a commotion at the doorway and two fellows crawled in dragging a stretcher […] it was an officer of the 8th Worcester who greeted me cheerily. "Where are you hit?" I asked. "In the back near the spine. Could you shift my gas helmet from under me?" I cut away the satchel and dragged it out; then he asked for a cigarette. Dunham produced one and he put it between his lips; I struck a match and held it across, but the cigarette had fallen on to his chest and he was dead.

'[…] I went out again into the open […] From the darkness on all sides came the groans and wails of wounded men; faint, long, sobbing moans of agony, and despairing shrieks. It was too horribly obvious that dozens of men with serious wounds must have crawled for safety into new shell-holes, and now the water was rising about them and, powerless to move, they were slowly drowning.

[…]

'The cries of the wounded had much diminished now, and as we staggered down the road, the reason was only too apparent, for the water was right over the tops of the shell-holes. [Men] lay groaning and blaspheming, and often we stopped to drag them up on to the ridges of earth. We lied to them all that the stretcher-bearers were coming.

[…]

'I hardly recognised [HQ] and at its entrance was a long mound of bodies […] a hand stretched out and clung to my equipment. Horrified I dragged a living man from amongst the corpses.

'[…] Doggedly driving all thought out of my head I bathed, crawled into bed […] and slept.

'At about 9 a.m. I dragged myself wearily out to take a muster parade on which my worst fears were realized […] Poor old Pepper had gone – hit in the back by a chunk of shell; twice buried as he lay dying in a hole, his dead body blown up and lost after Willis had carried it back […] Ewing hit by machine-gun bullets had lain beside him for a while and taken messages for his girl at home.

'Chalk, our little treasure, had been seen to fall riddled with bullets; then he too had been hit by a shell. Sergeant Wheeldon, DCM and bar, MM and bar, was killed and Foster. Also Corporal Harrison, Oldham, Mucklow and imperturbable McKay. My black sheep – Dawson and Taylor – had died together, and out of our happy little band of 90 men, only 15 remained.

'[…] So this was the end of 'D' Company. Feeling sick and lonely I returned to my tent to write out my casualty report; but instead I sat on the floor and drank whisky after whisky as I gazed into a black and empty future.'

Activites

Above reading and walking of the cemetery. This is a good site to see concrete bunkers, which largely became a feature of the German defences from 1917 onwards.

The four mourning figures sculpture by Emil Krieger.

5. Vancouver Corner – Brooding Soldier

5 minutes or deliver information to group on the coach as you drive past.

Turn right out of the Langemark cemetery car park and head south on Klerkenstraat. Continue on to Zonnebekestraat for 2km. As you come to a junction, the Brooding Soldier will emerge into view. Turn right and then immediately left. Parking for coaches available on the left.

Context

Beautiful Canadian Memorial to those who faced the 2nd Ypres gas attack.

Orientation

St Julian was a position in the north easterly section of the British part of the Salient. It saw very heavy fighting and was a complete waste land by the war's end.

Spiel

This is the Brooding Soldier at Vancouver corner. It is a monument built in honour of those Canadian soldiers, 18,000 of them, who encountered the first German gas attack here during 22-24 April 1915, 2,000 were killed.

This memorial was built in 1923. It is often admired as one of the best sculptures on the entire Western Front. The soldier mourns for the dead, but is rising out of the ground. It speaks of those lost, but yearns for a better future.

Activities

A small site to explore, if you have time.

6. Tyne Cot CWGC Cemetery

One hour minimum

Picking up from previous directions, turn left from the car park on to Zonnebekestraat. Drive 2km and turn left onto Roeselarestraat. Drive for just over 1km and turn right onto Schipstraat. Take the first left and pick up signs for Tyne Cot CWGC Cemetery. There is a large car park at the rear of the cemetery.

Context

The largest CWGC cemetery in the world.

Orientation

As you enter the cemetery, turn immediately right. Look out over the fields (so the cemetery is largely behind you) and you will see Ypres in the distance. You are looking out over the battlefield of Third Ypres.

Spiel

This is Tyne Cot cemetery; it is the largest British military cemetery in the world. There are 11,953 burials, 8,366, or nearly 70 per cent, are unknown. This gives some idea about the dreadful nature of the fighting that these men endured.

The name Tyne Cot is thought to derive from the fact that during Third Ypres the 50th (Northumbrian) Division fought here and gave some cottages nearby the name.[22]

Look out across the fields; five miles away you will see the spire of the Cloth Hall in Ypres. Just consider how good your view is here. You are standing in a German occupied and heavily fortified position from 1917. Look in the cemetery and you will see two pillboxes. There were five or six here in 1917. There is a third still on site, underneath

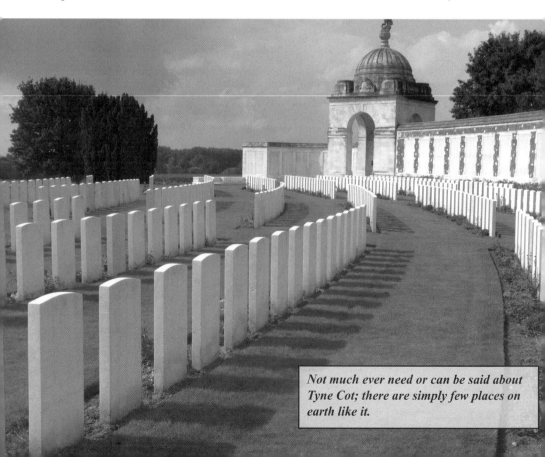

Not much ever need or can be said about Tyne Cot; there are simply few places on earth like it.

and incorporated into the Cross of Sacrifice at the suggestion of King George V, who visited in 1922 and surveyed the view you are looking at now. Pillboxes were strong points on a battlefield; they could withstand direct hits and offered substantial protection for those within, despite being seen as a magnet for artillery and therefore potential death traps by the troops themselves. As you have learnt, the Germans generally held the higher ground. It might only be a gentle slope, but here it is enough to control a considerable distance around.

Draw your eyes out across the fields again. Fix your view to approximately half way between here and Ypres. On 31 July this was the British front line and would be where Third Ypres would be launched from.

What you see in front of you was, during those three months of battle, hell. The heavy rain and constant shelling had turned the earth to a gloopy, oozing mess of decay and devastation. It was over this land that British and Commonwealth troops fought for three months before the Australians captured this position in October and the Canadians took Passchendaele ridge, about a mile from here, in November. Three and a half months, a few miles and 285,000 British and Commonwealth casualties. The Germans suffered approximately the same number.

The view from the raised Cross of Sacrifice, looking out across the cemetery and over the infamous Third Ypres battleground.

Walking Tyne Cot is a pilgrimage and a pleasure. At the same time one can feel both utterly horrified and yet uplifted; it is difficult to explain until visited.

This cemetery can be too much for some.

Make your way slowly through the rows and try to pick out an individual grave. There are burials here from across the whole of the British Front. The first burials were made in 1917 and are behind the cross.

At the back of the cemetery is the Tyne Cot Memorial which lists the names of those British soldiers who fought and died in the Salient between August 1917 to the end of the war and whose bodies were not found, and therefore have no known grave. The reason for the dates commemorated is due to the fact that originally all those without a grave were to be listed on the Menin Gate in Ypres. The Menin Gate ran out of space. There are 34,927 names listed on the memorial panels here. However, all Canadian and Australian missing are on the Menin Gate.

Activities

Walk the cemetery, view the battlefield from the cross of sacrifice and view the memorial.[23]

Return to your coach, head back in to Ypres and eat dinner![24]

7. Menin Gate and Last Post Ceremony

Begins at 2000 every night. I suggest that you have your group there by 1945 at the latest; numbers attending have increased dramatically recently. The ceremony itself will last approximately ten minutes.

If you (and/or a few of your students) would like to take part in the ceremony (I would whole-heartedly recommend it) by way of placing a wreath, then log on to

Buglers from the local fire brigade sounding the Last Post at the Menin Gate.

www.lastpost.be and click on the ceremonies tab and participation option. This will need to be done several weeks at least before you travel.

Context

The memorial to the missing of the Salient and the Last Post.

Orientation

During the war, British soldiers, heading to the northern and eastern parts of the Salient, left Ypres by way of this break in the ramparts across a bridge and towards the front line.

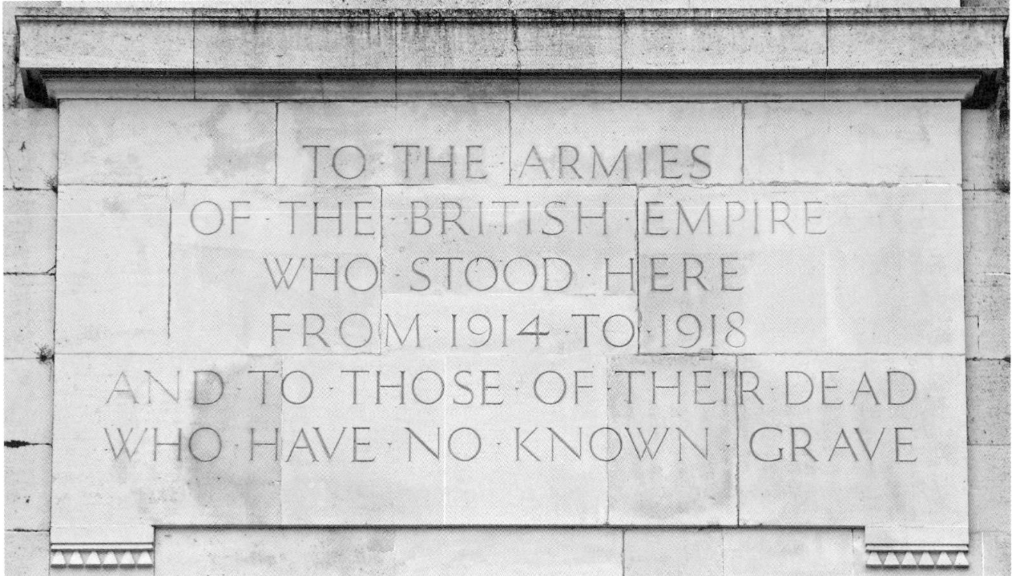

Inscription on the Menin Gate.

Spiel

Every day since 1928, apart from four years during the German occupation of the Second World War, just before eight o'clock in the evening, the traffic is stopped from passing through the Menin Gate and buglers march into the road and face the town.[25] They then play the Last Post, usually followed by the laying of wreaths, The Exhortation and Reveille. It is one of the simplest and most moving few minutes you are ever likely to experience. This is a tribute to the fallen. Even if others around you do, do not applaud at the end of the ceremony.

It was quickly decided that a Memorial to the Missing of the Salient would be needed following the war. This site was chosen for its symbolic importance, not just in the war itself as the passage through which soldiers travelled on their way to the front, but as a monument to Britain and her Empire and what was endured and achieved here.

The Menin Gate was designed by Sir Reginald Blomfield and has inscribed upon it the names of 54,332 men who died or who are missing in the Salient, for the British up to 15 August 1917, and who have no known grave. On 24 July 1927, Field Marshal Plumer, as he then was, opened the memorial and spoke directly to the hundreds of relatives in attendance and to the millions of others around the world when he said this of their lost loved ones: 'He is not missing. He is here.'

Whilst the ceremony takes place, focus on a single name on a panel and reflect on everything that you have experienced today.

DAY END

To see the vast numbers who attend the ceremony, regardless of the time of year or the weather, is inspirational in itself.

Day Two Itinerary

Approximate start time of 0830 and finish between 1200-1400. When designing this day's itinerary I have in mind it being your final day of the tour. Therefore, I have made it a half day, assuming that you would be departing for onward transport back to the UK at some point in the afternoon. It is also a less intense day, in general, than Day One in Ypres. If you just did the four main visits then you would probably be finished by 1200. If you did all of the additional ones then you can add two hours. It would be relatively straight forward to add another couple of visits (see suggested extra Ypres visits at the end of this itinerary) to make it a full day, if required.

1. **Messines Church**
2. **Island of Ireland Peace Park**
    - 2a. Pool of Peace
    - 2b. Bayernwald Trench System
    - 2c. Hill 60
3. **Flanders Fields Museum**
4. **Ramparts Walk**

1. Messines Church

20 minutes

Messines (Mesen) can be easily reached by taking the N366/N365 south out of Ypres. After approximately 10km you will reach the smallest city in Belgium. You can park in the central square. From there, you will be able to see the church spire – walk to the church.

Context

Good views of the battlefield from this German strongpoint and a link to future men of high importance!

Orientation

As you look at the entrance to the church, there is a grassed area to the right. You will see a semi-circular orientation table. This is a good place to gather and from here you are looking from the German position, prior to Third Ypres in 1917, towards the British lines. The contrast in tactical placement is stark! This is a good place to talk before heading into the Church.

Spiel

- An overview of the Battle of Messines, 1917 (page 78)

Then:

This church was wiped from the map by the end of the war but was rebuilt in 1928 to a smaller scale. It was very much in safe German territory, on the strongpoint of the Messines Ridge. One part of the church remains original however: the crypt.[26] This was a particularly good place for German soldiers to shelter during a heavy bombardment or to receive medical treatment. One German corporal speaks of the inner turmoil of a soldier and of the fighting endured in Flanders:

> 'The time came when everyone had to fight between the instinct of self-preservation and the admonition of duty. I, too, was not spared this inner struggle. Whenever death was on the hunt, an undefinable something tried to revolt, tried to present itself to the weak body in the form of reason [...] but the more this voice tried to warn me [...] the sharper was my resistance.'

And, during combat:

> 'suddenly an iron salute came whizzing over our heads towards us and with a sharp report the small bullets struck between our rows, whipping up the wet earth; but before the small cloud had dispersed, out of two hundred throats the first hurrah roared a welcome to the first messenger of death. But then it began to crackle and roar, to sing and howl [...] the fight of man

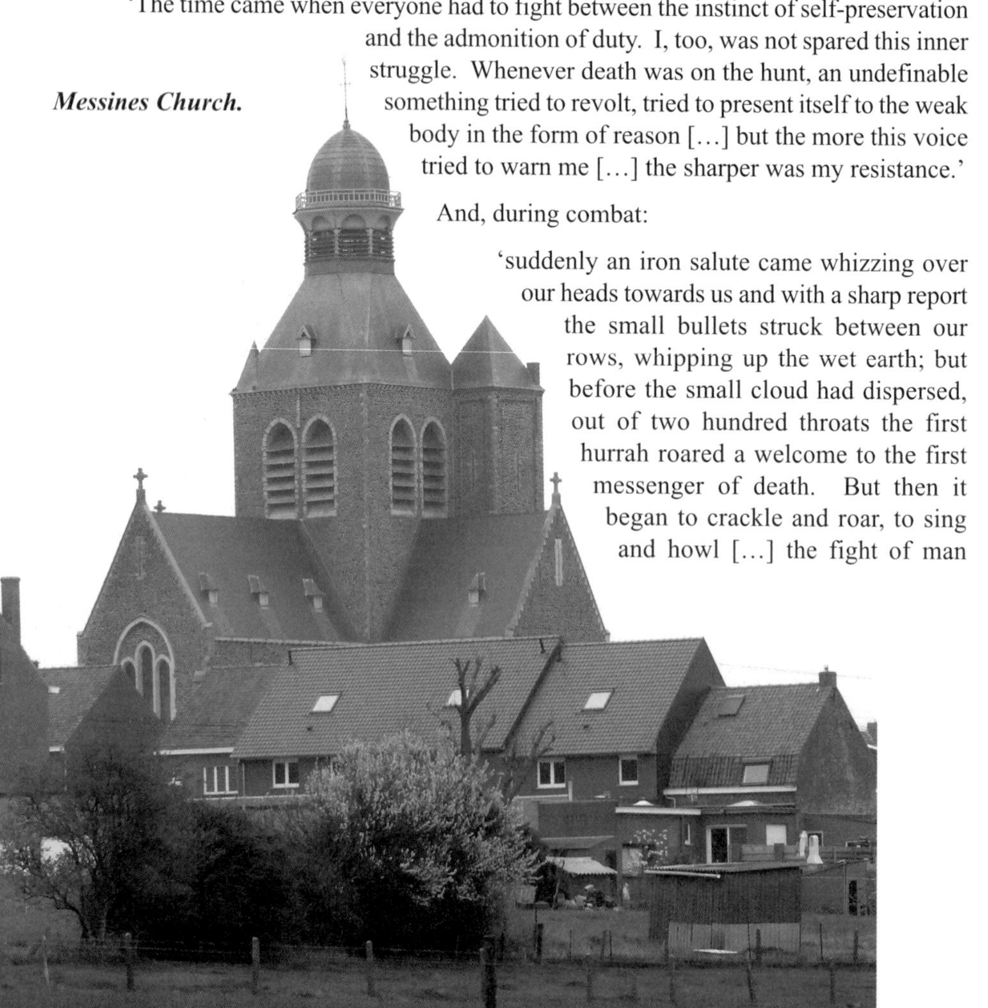

Messines Church.

against man. But from the distance the sounds of a song [...] Deutschland, Deutschland, über alles.'[27]

This was Corporal Adolf Hitler of the 16th Bavarian Reserve Infantry Regiment. Hitler volunteered in 1914, won the Iron Cross First and Second Class and served in Ypres during the first and third battles. He was ostensibly a runner, delivering messages between the front and rear lines; a dangerous job that had a very high casualty rate. He was, famously, back in Germany, recuperating from the effects of a gas attack, when he learned of the armistice. He would forever believe that the German Army had been "stabbed in the back" by Jewish power-brokers and politicians and would make it his life's work to overturn the Treaty of Versailles that had neutered Germany following the First World War.[28]

He also received medical treatment in the crypt of this church.

Before we enter the crypt, one final point: Corporal Hitler was here in 1915 and, in January 1916, a recently chastened politician served in the trench system just a couple of kilometres to the south (Ploegsteert), as a battalion commander. His name was Winston Churchill.

Enter the church and head to the front of the seating area. The entrance to the crypt is down a flight of stairs to your right. There is only enough space for ten to fifteen people at a time. Do encourage your group to sign the visitor book and leave a small donation for the church.

The crypt containing the tomb of Countess Adela, William the Conqueror's mother in law.

2. Island of Ireland Peace Park

20 minutes

Take the N365 out of Messines and towards Ploegsteert. Within a minute the large tower of the Peace Park will be seen on your right.

Context

Peace tower and park commemorating *all* of Ireland's war history.

Orientation

The attack here, on 7 June 1917, came from the west (to the rear of the site) and headed east. It was actually New Zealand troops who captured this particular area; the site was chosen due to the fact that soldiers from both the 16th (Irish) Division and the 36th (Ulster) Division fought side by side near to this ground at the other end of the ridge, in front of Wytschaete. As you look down the slope you will see Petite Douve Farm and a bunker in the grounds. Under the farm is an abandoned mine from the Messines Ridge battle.[29]

Spiel

Following the tumultuous events in Ireland both during and after the First World War, not least of course the Easter Rebellion uprising in 1916, the commemoration of the role of Irish soldiers in the war became dangerously entwined with the politics of the island.

After the partition of Ireland in 1922, many soldiers from the Catholic south, who had volunteered and fought on the side of the "enemy", were treated as pariahs or even traitors by their communities. In Northern Ireland, the exact opposite was true and one of the first memorials built on the Western Front was the Ulster Tower on the Somme, in 1921 –

The impressive tower at the Island of Ireland Peace Park.

here was the flag flying for the Protestant north. If one travels down the Shankill Road in Belfast today, you will see numerous murals on the sides of houses commemorating Ulstermen and the Somme.

However, in reality, the Great War was a story of unity for the Irish, at least for those fighting in the war. It was near this site that men from the 16th (Irish) Division and the 36th (Ulster) Division fought side by side and not against one another.

This tower and the surrounding park were built to honour that unity. It is of a traditional Irish design, made with stone from Tipperary and Mullingar.[30] At 1100 on 11 November the tower is specially designed to be illuminated inside by the sun's rays.

On 11 November 1998 the park was formally opened. In attendance were Queen Elizabeth II, King Albert II of Belgium and the Irish President, Mary McAleese, who spoke the following moving words:

> 'For much of the past eighty years, the very idea of such a ceremony would probably have been unthinkable.
>
> Those whom we commemorate here were doubly tragic. They fell victim to a war against oppression in Europe. Their memory, too, fell victim to a war for independence at home in Ireland.'

There are various points of interest throughout the park. You will find memorials to those killed, wounded or missing, tablets to the counties of Ireland, explanations of the battle area and many wonderfully moving selections of prose. Here is one for you, explore the rest:

> 'As it was, the Ypres battleground just represented one gigantic slough of despond into which floundered battalions, brigades and divisions of infantry without end to

be shot to pieces or drowned, until at last and with immeasurable slaughter we had gained a few miles of liquid mud.'

- Charles Miller, 2nd Royal Inniskilling Fusilliers

2a. The Pool of Peace, Spanbroekmolen

20 minutes

Return to Messines on the N365; at the northern end, at a crossroads, turn left on the N314. Take the first right on to Kruisstraat for approximately 2km. You will pass Lone Tree CWGC Cemetery on your left and the Pool of Peace will be just after on your right (note: small parking area, so can be tricky in a large coach).

Context

1917 mine crater, now a symbol of peace and tranquillity

From carnage to tranquility.

Orientation

The mine was blown underneath one of the highest German points in front of the Messines Ridge. The British advanced from the direction of Lone Tree Cemetery.

Spiel

This is the site of the largest of the nineteen mines which were fired under German strong points as part of the Messines Ridge campaign on 7 June, 1917. Chaplain William Doyle, of the 16th (Irish) Division, recorded the moments the mines blew:

> 'The guns had ceased firing, to give their crews a breathing space before the storm of battle broke; for a moment at least there was peace on earth and a calm which was almost more trying than the previous roar to us who knew what was coming. A prisoner told us that the enemy knew we were about to attack, but did not expect it for another couple of days. I pictured to myself our men, row upon row waiting in the darkness for the word to charge, and on the other side the Germans in their trenches and dug-outs, little thinking that [...] huge mines were laid under their feet, needing only a spark to blow them into eternity. The tension of waiting was terrific, the strain almost unbearable. One felt inclined to scream out and send them warning. But all I could do was to stand on top of the trench and give them Absolution, trusting to God's mercy to speed it so far.
>
> 'Even now I can scarcely think of the scene which followed without trembling with horror. Punctually to the second at 3.10 a.m. there was a deep muffled roar; the ground in front of where I stood rose up, as if some giant had wakened from his sleep and was bursting his way through the earth's crust, and then I saw seven huge columns of smoke and flames shoot hundreds of feet into the air, while masses of clay and stones, tons in weight, were hurled about like pebbles. I never before realized what an earthquake was like, for not only did the ground quiver and shake, but actually rocked backwards and forwards, so that I kept on my feet with difficulty.
>
> 'Later on I examined one of the mine craters, an appalling sight, for I knew that many a brave man, torn and burnt by the explosion, lay buried there.'[31]

There was, however, a minor problem with the mine here at Spanbroelmolen. Eighteen mines blew at 0310. The nineteenth, this one, blew fifteen seconds late. A number of soldiers of the Royal Irish Rifles, having left their trench at 0310, may well have been

killed by the explosion or the falling debris of their own mine. Many are buried in Lone Tree Cemetery, across the road from here.

In order to preserve it as a memory of the fallen and to be a symbol for future peace, Lord Wakefield, of Toc H fame, bought this site in 1930 and it was christened the Pool of Peace.

Activities

A moment's reflection and/or poetry reading. A visit to Lone Tree Cemetery; this may well take 15 minutes.

2b. Bayernwald German Trench System

30-45 minutes

With the Pool of Peace to your right, continue on the road until you come to a T junction. Turn left on to the N304 toward Kemmel. Follow the signs for Kemmel and park up as near to the central square as you can.

You should follow the (clear) signs for the information office to pay for and pick up your entry tickets to the trench system. Only one person in the group need do this; the rest can wait on the bus. Alternatively, your tour company may be able to arrange tickets before travel. The cost is exceptional at only €1 for those under 26 years of age. Once collected you head for the trench system (approximately ten minutes from Kemmel). The tourist information office will give you directions and they are printed on the reverse of the entrance tickets. It is advisable to walk the final stretch to the trench entrance.

Context

Outstanding, recently excavated and restored section of German trench. Reputedly a section where Hitler served.

The Bayernwald trench system is one of the best sites to understand German positional strength in the Salient.

... it is also a large and intriguing site to explore.

Orientation

Excellent for understanding the tactical positioning of the Germans; Ypres can be clearly overlooked from here.

Spiel

This position was taken by the Germans in 1914 and trench systems were constructed here shortly after. The Allies called this position Croonaert Wood, but the Germans, named after the mighty Bavarian units first stationed here, called it Bayernwald or Bavarian Wood.

It was near to here that Adolf Hitler won an Iron Cross; he almost certainly walked this trench system. On his tour of 1940, he visited here too; again another example of the shadow which this war cast over him.

This area was painstakingly restored under strict archaeological conditions and the current trenches are that of a 1916 system. You will notice the trench sides are made of woven wickerwork branches, unlike those of the Allied systems. There are four concrete dugouts and a mineshaft. Explore the dugouts and consider them for a moment; these were built to grant temporary shelter from artillery fire, they were far from comfortable and that was the point – the soldier should be at his post as soon as possible.

From this position, one can also gain an understanding of the positions which the Germans held in the Salient. Ypres can be not just seen, but monitored from here. This is one of the finest examples of German strength in Flanders that you can still experience today.

Activities

Explore the trenches. Note how easy it is to lose all sense of direction.

A superb view inside the trench works at Bayernwald.

2c. Hill 60

30-40 mins

This is dependent on where you have been able to park. There is a shorter route from Bayernwald, but it is not really suitable for coaches. If travelling by coach then you should follow signs to Wijtschate and, once there, pick up signs for the N365 towards Ypres. Keep on this, heading over the roundabout, for approximately 5.5km before taking the right hand turn on to Komenseweg. Travel on this road for 3.3km before turning left on to Zwarteleenstraat. Hill 60 is signposted.

Context

An artificially created high point, in an area of flat land, which was bitterly contested throughout the war and became synonymous with the tunnelling and mining aspect of the war. Preserved in its pock marked state, with bunkers and memorials.

Orientation

You are standing on a low rise at the south east of the Salient. This position changed hands numerous times during the war. When not in their hands, German positions were to the south and east.

Spiel

Hill 60 is not really a hill at all. This sixty metres of high ground was made before the war from the earth dug for the Ypres-Comines railway line. Although far from a towering mountain, this was actually the highest place in the area and thus its importance cannot be underestimated.

In late 1914 the French lost these positions to the Germans, who now used them for excellent observation of Ypres and to direct artillery bombardment upon that fated city. The British made its recapture a priority.

It was Major J. Norton Griffiths, a remarkable figure – millionaire, MP, adventurer – who convinced Secretary of War Kitchener that the tactics required were those of mining. Griffiths had made his fortune from constructing underground tunnel networks for pipes and cables in British cities and he would employ the same techniques on the Western Front – no heavy machinery or drilling, this tunnelling would be carried out by the clay-kickers.

Griffiths, understanding that Ypres soil was predominantly clay, had been extolling the virtues of his plan to bemused senior army personnel since late 1914. It took the mining activities of the German army and the psychological fear of being blown to nothing, which was beginning to grip the British soldiers in early 1915, which finally won Griffiths his argument. Clay kickers were recruited and shipped out to the front, all within a week, in February 1915. The Underground War was underway.[32]

Clay kicking was a process where the individual crawled into a small tunnel and lay on "the cross" – a piece of wood which tilted one at 45 degrees. Using spades tied to their feet, the clay kicker then painstakingly went to work, scraping and digging clay out

Concrete pillbox, Hill 60.

to be removed into sandbags and taken out of the tunnel. The clay kicker worked in dangerous, filthy conditions – not to mention the claustrophobia and fear of German counter mining. More traditional mining methods were used across the Western Front, developing complex underground systems at numerous points along the line.

At Hill 60, a shaft was dug down an initial sixteen feet and then the tunnellers began their work, advancing ten to fifteen feet per day. This was a hellish, mole-like existence; at times men would black out, be buried alive or break into German tunnels and have to engage in hand to hand combat in cramped conditions – it was not unknown for men to have to claw and grasp, strangle and stab, all in the belly of the earth itself.

Yet, by 17 April the tunnels were complete and the explosives readied. At 1900 the charge was fired and in an instant over a hundred Germans were obliterated, as was much of the now-not-so-Hill-like Hill 60. An artillery bombardment and then bayonet charge followed. Only seven British Soldiers were killed in the initial fighting as opposed to the much heavier German losses.

The Memorial to 1 Australian Tunnelling Company at Hill 60 (with accompanying bullet holes; scars of the Second World War).

Remember that you are standing on their graves, they – and their successors – still lie here.

Almost immediately the Germans counter attacked and fighting continued here throughout the war: the Germans recaptured it on 5 May 1916, the British retook it during the Messines campaign on June 7 1917, the Germans once again occupying it during the Kaiser's offensive in April 1918, before its final capture by the British on 28 September 1918. Hill 60 is itself a monument to the fury, effort and carnage of the war. Thousands died here, thousands are still here.

One final point, during the early days of the Second World War, fighting returned to Hill 60. The bunkers came out of their retirement. Outside the main site you will find a memorial to 1 Australian Tunnelling Company, complete with bullet holes from the Second World War. The Germans also destroyed the original monument to the Queen Victoria's Rifles because of the reference to the German first use of gas on the inscription.

Activities

Explore the bunkers, site, memorials and information panels.

3. In Flanders Fields Museum

1-1.5 hours

Head back to Ypres. The museum is located in the Cloth Hall itself.

Pre-book online at http://www.inflandersfields.be/en

Price: €4 for those part of a school group. €8 full adult price.

Context

Recently redesigned and inter-active museum.

Spiel

If not already done, then before entering describe what was left of Ypres after the war and its subsequent rebuilding. *(Page 79)*

Activity

Museum visit. The museum is one of those where you could easily spend four hours or, as I have seen many students do, rush round in twenty minutes. Strategic placing of staff and a 'guiding hand' would be advisable!

Factor lunch in before or after and it is also a good opportunity to provide some free shopping time in town. If you take your group, as a whole, to the Leonidas chocolate shop on the main square, he will give you some fantastic deals (and freebies for the staff!). It is best to arrange this beforehand; if you are staying in Ypres, then drop in one of the days before or ask your hotel to let them know. If you are just visiting for the day, then e-mail them on info@chocolatesdegroote.be

Ramparts CWGC Cemetery, a favourite of the great Rose Coombs.

4. Ramparts Walk

45 minutes

Leave the Cloth Hall and walk to the Menin Gate. As you reach the Menin Gate, walk up the incline to the right, which will bring you out on top of the ramparts. You are going to follow this pathway for 20-30 minutes until you reach Ramparts Cemetery. Enter the cemetery when you reach it. Before you begin the walk, make sure that you have arranged with your coach driver to pick you up at Lille Gate, rather than you walking back into town.

Context

A fitting end to your pilgrimage!

Spiel

We have just walked the remaining sections of Vauban ramparts which once surrounded the city of Ypres. In the casemates and chambers below, the British army ran signallers' stations, HQs and shelters. It was in one of these casemates that the *Wipers Times* was written and published, using an old printing press that some soldiers had located early in the war.

This is Ramparts Cemetery; it is one of the smaller cemeteries on the Western Front, with just 198 graves. It is also one of the most peaceful and beautiful. These soldiers will spend their eternity looking out across the calm of the moat, a calm that bears no resemblance to the horror they witnessed. If one were to don scuba gear and dive into that moat, and it is said that some of the owners of the souvenir shops in Ypres do just that, and swam to the bottom, then you would be reunited with the war. The Iron Harvest of shrapnel and bullets are in there and are testament to the battering that Ypres withstood.

This cemetery was the favourite of one of the most famous battlefield authors and guides, a lady named Rose Coombs, who worked for a long time at the Imperial War Museum. In fact, that walk you have just taken is named the Rose Coombs Walk in her honour. When she passed away in 1991, her ashes were scattered here; a rose bush marks that spot.

This is our final visit of the trip. You will have you own memories, thoughts and emotions. Think of those individuals, stories and places that have made an impression. You have been on a pilgrimage. What you have done is so important to keeping the memory of the fallen of the Great War alive.

Thank you.

Activites

Moment of reflection whilst walking the cemetery.

Leave the cemetery and descend to street level (follow the signs for Lille Gate). Embark on your coach and head for onward connection back to Blighty.

TOUR END

* * *

Additional Ypres Salient Visits

Below are ideas for extra visits to add to your tour if you are looking to extend it by up to another full day. I have given a brief description and an idea of where they would naturally fit, geographically, on the previous two days.

Polygon Wood CWGC Cemetery/Buttes CWGC Cemetery/New Zealand Memorial – Day One after 2a.

Visit the replanted wood and, in particular, Buttes New British Cemetery, which includes the beautiful New Zealand memorial. This was very much a front line position throughout the war.

Passchendaele 1917 Museum, Zonnebeke – Day One after 5 or 6

http://www.passchendaele.be/eng/museumEN.html. An excellent museum, recently substantially expanded.

Ploegsteert Memorial and Last Post – Day Two after 2

Visit the rotunda memorial to the missing, guarded by two prominent lions, and attached cemeteries. It was near here that Winston Churchill served in the trenches. The Last Post is sounded here at 1900 on the first Friday of the month.

Kemmel Hill, French Memorial and French National Cemetery – Day Two after 2

An area of much importance, particularly during the 1918 Spring Offensive, when a massive German assault wrested control of the hill from the French. This highpoint can be seen from most sections of the Ypres battlefield.

Lettenberg Bunkers – Day Two after 2

British underground HQ and troop accommodation. It was from here that British officers watched the action of the Messines Ridge campaign unfold.

* * *

Footnotes:

1. Perhaps as you enjoy a refreshing Duvel or Jupiler in the Grote Market after a day's battlefield touring, you might like to muse not just on the Tommies whose footsteps you are walking but also those, like Napoleon, who have been to this place too. In 1940, Adolf Hitler, upon the capitulation of French forces, travelled across France and Belgium to meet with many of his generals and to visit sites of interest to him from the First World War. On 1 June he visited Ypres and walked through the Menin Gate. The huge beer industry was largely a consequence of the collapse of the medieval wool trade.
2. Nineteen mines were blown, five were not used and one was abandoned. One exploded in 1955 during a thunderstorm, killing a cow, near Plugstreet, where there are three others as part of the Bird Cage cluster. Another is under La Petite Douve Farm, south of the Island of Ireland Peace Park; this one was found by the Germans and abandoned by the British. Another is by Peckham.
3. Focused artillery bombardment on specific German defences, across a much shorter section of front, followed by infantry advance and sustained defence of newly captured positions before beginning the next stage of assault, allowing guns to be brought forward for a new assault.
4. This may be as high as 450,000 Allied and 410,000 German.
5. Remember that with the entry into the war of the United States, the Allies had potentially a ready supply of millions of new troops on the horizon. The German army was becoming perilously devoid of quality soldiers. In essence, the Allies could afford high casualty rates, the Germans could not.
6. You may come across reference to a Fifth Battle of Ypres, 28 September – 2 October, 1918. This was part of the Allied drive to victory and a plan put into operation by the newly installed Generalissimo of the Allied Armies, Marshal Ferdinand Foch. However, it was short lived and halted for a while (no surprises!) due to bad weather. Some action continued on until mid-October. Generally, it is not recognised by most historians as the

Fifth Battle – given its relatively slight duration; the battle as a part of the general Advance in Flanders, September to November 1918, is a more apt designation.

7. In the case of St Martin's, the spire was made significantly higher than that of the original.
8. These timings are a rough guide and do not include any travel time between stops.
9. This museum is somewhat controversial in the battlefield tours community. Some guides are unhappy with the entrance fee. However, for the first time visitor, this place still delivers the best example of what it was 'really like' and those of us who pride ourselves on being 'experts' probably need to remember that and cease our pomposity!
10. i.e. they could have been reinforced for defensive purposes, then additional trenches added, then a need to alter line of sight, then captured and defences reversed… etc, etc. You get the point: trench warfare could be confusing and it is appropriate that it still confuses us now.
11. Certainly not at all German positions, however. Concrete bunkers were only really present on any large scale from 1917 onwards. Many German soldiers would not agree that they lived in luxury!
12. (Van Emden, 2005, p. 102.) Given the nature of this book I have endeavoured to limit the number of direct citations so that they do not get in the way. Only when I have quoted at length, or wish to pass on a particular piece of information from another source, have I used them. All details of the sources which I have consulted (and would recommend to the reader) are referenced in full at the end of this book.
13. A useful time to speak to the group on the coach microphone, explaining the significance of the journey you are now making – i.e. away from the front line, back toward Ypres and then towards the relative safety of Poperinge. You are making the journey that many Tommies hoped they would get to make when they were stationed at the front!
14. (Luard, 1930)
15. Other criteria are accepted too; but in the case of this example the soldiers will have died on active service and their relatives will have taken up the option of repatriation and burial.
16. (Campion Vaughan, 1982, pp. 184-185) To my mind, the best memoir of the war.
17. Nine times out of ten this is open; however, inexplicably – or so it seems – it can be closed. Be prepared that you might be unlucky. Also, sometimes the doors are closed but not locked, so do make sure that you try them!
18. Thirty-five murderers were shot, such as C.C. Wang of the Chinese Labour Corps, who was executed here on 08/05/1919. In 2012 a new, non-original, post replaced one that had been in the courtyard for many years. The previous one was thought to be that to which Wang was tied.
19. Though not the youngest soldier buried in the Salient. John Condon is buried in Poelkapelle Cemetery and is listed as being 14 years of age. However, this is disputed. There are claims that he was 18, that the body buried there is not him and there are counter claims that he was actually 13!
20. In a most moving visit to Langemark, one of my students (a boy from England) had a German relative buried in the pit. In recent years work has been done to identify the soldiers in this mass grave and so far 17,000 have been named. If you are interested, the boy's relative was called Heuck and you will find him on the panel. It was a remarkably sobering moment.

21. A selection from the brilliant *Some Desperate Glory* (Campion Vaughan, 1982), pages 221-232. I urge you to buy this book. The above reading will take approximately ten minutes; this may seem like a long time to hold a group's attention but I have never read this and not had the group in absolute silence, waiting on every single word. When you finish reading, I would recommend just walking away from the group and meeting them back at the coach; hugely powerful. Also, the names that Vaughan mention above can be found, along with many more, on Panel 23 to 28 and 163A of the Tyne Cot Memorial.
22. A much disputed claim. The cottages were long destroyed by 1917 and Tyne Cot appeared on British trench maps as a term for the area before then too. Some speculation suggests that there was lettering on an old barn or that it was named after the river by British map-makers; all is conjecture.
23. I have taken the decision to leave out an individual story to tell at Tyne Cot, simply because there are so many and, by this stage of a long day, many of your group will want some quiet time to walk the cemetery and think through the day (and they may be sick of your voice!). If you would like a story then one of the most often told is that of the Moorhouses and it is of personal importance to the author as both were old boys of the school I attended. Lieutenant Colonel Harry Moorhouse was in command of the 1/4th Bn KOYLI. His son, Ronald, was a captain in the same unit. Ronald was shot leading an attack on 9 October. He was brought back to HQ where his father insisted on trying to find a doctor to treat him. As he left his dugout, Harry was shot and killed. Both father and son died within half an hour of each other. You can find their names on panel 108-111.
24. Do make sure that this is pre-booked by yourself or your tour company. I have eaten at numerous locations in central Ypres with school groups and have never had a bad meal. An ideal time to book for would be 1800 or 1830.
25. Until the 1980s timings were 2000 in winter months and 2100 in summer months.
26. The church was originally founded by Countess Adela in 1057 and it is she who is buried in the crypt. Her marriage to Baldwin V of Flanders would produce a daughter, Mathilde, who would go on to marry… William "the Conqueror", Duke of Normandy.
27. Both taken from the 1941 American print version of Adolf Hitler's *Mein Kampf*, pp 213-215.
28. The Treaty (1919) limited the German Army to 100,000 men, forbade an Airforce and union with Austria, limited the size of the Navy and took land and overseas possessions. Germany also had to pay £6.6 billion (a reduced figure from the original, according to one index now worth £22 billion) the much adjusted figure was finally paid off on 23 October 2010.
29. It always intrigues me as to what the farmer's insurance bill looks like!
30. In a startling coincidence, Mullingar is the home town of Lieutenant Maurice Dease, first VC winner of the war. He is buried in St Symphorien CWGC Cemetery in Mons.
31. See http://fatherdoyle.com/ for more on the life of this remarkable man. Doyle was killed during Third Ypres on 16 August 1917.
32. I am indebted to Winston Groom for bringing Griffith's story to my attention in the brilliant *A Storm in Flanders* (see further reading), upon which I have based much of this Hill 60 information.

Tour Three:

Going Further: Mons, Arras, Loos and Neuve Chapelle

An introduction to sites beyond Ypres and the Somme

The vast majority of visitors to the Western Front visit Ypres and the battlefields of the Somme; few venture beyond these areas. For me, some of the very best sites are to be found in other locations and, if one truly wants to get a grasp of how and where the war started, its ebbs and flows and ultimate end, then you have to go further afield.

This, much smaller, section is simply meant to fire your interest for further travel and acts as an introduction to Mons, Arras, Loos and Neuve Chapelle. It provides an outline itinerary for a one day visit encompassing all of these locations. If you choose to follow this exactly, then be prepared for a heavy and busy schedule! Covering the sites in one day is possible – I have done it with a group of forty people in tow – but if you have more time then you could spread these visits over several days by going to the extra visits, marked with an *.

I have also assumed that if you are reading this chapter, and considering going beyond the usual Western Front tourist routes of the previous chapters, then you are comfortably versed in the history of the war, or at least inspired to carry out wider reading beyond this short book. Therefore, rather than setting out this chapter in the paint-by-numbers style of the previous two, I have stripped it back to a simple paragraph of detail for each stop.

However you choose to use this next section, I hope it intrigues you enough to make the short journeys required to discover a whole new perspective on the Great War. The visits are ideal for both large parties and the individual visitor. Visits to Mons and Arras work particularly well with school parties.

One-Day Itinerary

*The assumption made when planning this route is that the traveller is travelling south (perhaps from an overnight stay in Ypres or straight from a port such as Zeebrugge and wishes to head back north, perhaps back to Ypres, for the evening). Those with an * are extra visits beyond what is possible to fit in in one day. If you want to visit all of the sites below, then two days are much more realistic.*

1. **Mons:**
    - Nimy Canal Railway Bridge
    - First and Last Shots*
    - Town Centre*
    - St Symphorien CWGC Military Cemetery
2. **Arras:**
    - Town Centre*
    - Wellington Quarry
    - Arras Memorial*
    - Mur des Fusilles*
    - Vimy Ridge
    - Cabaret Rouge CWGC Cemetery*
    - Notre Dame de Lorette French National Cemetery*
3. **Loos:**
    - Dud Corner CWGC Cemetery and Loos Memorial
    - St Mary's ADS CWGC Cemetery*
4. **Neuve Chapelle:**
    - Portuguese Cemetery and Memorial*
    - Indian Memorial
    - Le Touret Memorial and CWGC Cemetery
5. **Fromelles:**
    - Pheasant Wood CWGC Cemetery

Giving some 'spiel' at Mons Canal.

Mons

History

This was the first action of the British Expeditionary Force in the war. British soldiers came into contact with men of the German army on 23 August 1914 at the Mons-Condé Canal. Despite valiant efforts, and inflicting heavy loss of life on the Germans, the BEF engaged in a long and wearying retreat to conform to the movement of the French on the right, ultimately to the outskirts of Paris, before pushing back against the thrusting force of the German invasion at the Battle of the Marne. Mons was not just where the war began for the BEF, but also where it ended, with the last shots fired by the British here in 1918.

Visits

Nimy Canal Railway Bridge

This is where the first significant fighting occurred between the two sides, with the British desperately attempting to halt the German advance and prevent them crossing the canal. On this bridge, rebuilt a second time after it was destroyed in the

The monkey of Mons; give it a rub for good luck!

St Symphorien CWGC New Military Cemetery.

Second World War, Lieutenant Maurice Dease and his men held up the Germans using two machine guns on the bridge. He was shot three times and eventually died. With only one gun now operational, Private Sidney Godley scrambled to take over the position. For over an hour he held up the German attack, despite being shot in the head, thus allowing the rest of the men to retreat. Finally, on the verge of being overrun, he smashed up the gun and attempted to limp off to safety, but was caught by the Germans and put in a prisoner of war camp. He survived the war. Both Dease and Godley were awarded the VC, with Dease's recognised as the first action of the war which resulted in the award of this highest honour.

First and Last Shots Memorials

Located on the N6, Rue Grande, these plaques commemorate the first and last British shots of the war; they are just yards apart, on opposite sides of a very busy road, near SHAPE.

Town Centre

Definitely worth a visit, if just for some personal refuelling! Dotted around the Grand

The stories of some of those who lay at rest in St Symphorien help you to understand the entire Western Front in just one cemetery. It is a remarkable place.

Place are numerous eateries. Many men of the BEF spent twenty four hours awaiting orders in this square, prior to 23 August 1914. A must find is the iron monkey, outside the Town Hall; this medieval curiosity is supposed to bring good luck to those who rub its head – and for those who tut at such things, do it anyway and think about the hundreds, if not thousands, of Tommies who did it in 1914.

St Symphorien CWGC New Military Cemetery

The author's favourite cemetery on the entire Western Front. It is unlike all other cemeteries, largely due to the fact that it was begun in 1914 by the Germans. Therefore, it contains a mixture of German and Commonwealth burials, most notably: Maurice Dease, of Nimy Bridge fame, Private J. Parr (first British soldier killed in the war), Private G.E. Ellison (last British soldier killed in the war), Private J.L. Price (last Commonwealth soldier killed in the war) and a German, Musketeer Oskar Niemeyer, who jumped into the Mons canal and swam across to the other side to operate a swing bridge that could bring his company across – he was successful but died carrying it out. All these graves can be located using the information in the registers at the entrance to the cemetery. Due to it being a symbol of shared grieving and the importance of the burials contained within, this cemetery was selected to be the site for the opening event of the British centenary remembrance programme in August 2014.

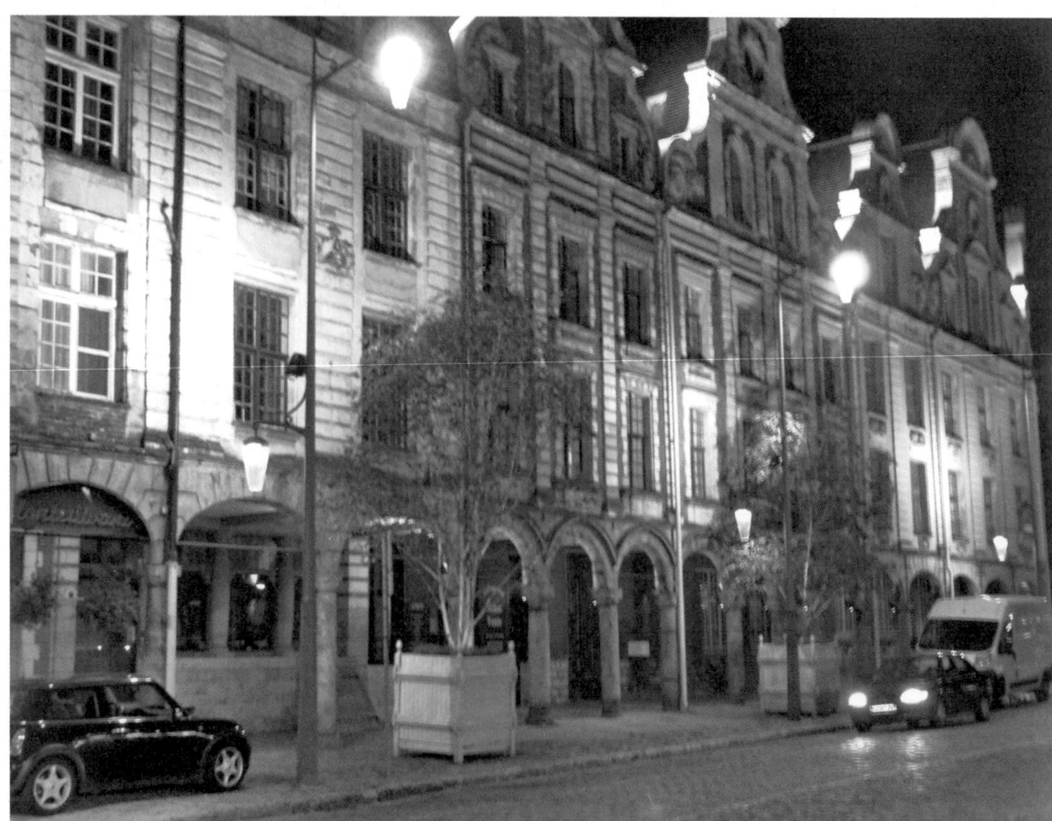

Arras, a pretty spot for some R&R.

Arras

History

Arras was near the front and was particularly active in 1915 (two major French offensives), in spring 1917 (Battle of Arras) and the German Spring Offensive of 1918. The city itself was severely damaged and nearly all of what you see has been rebuilt since. The British held the city from early 1916. Between 9 April and 16 May 1917 the British fought a major offensive in this sector, best known for the capture of Vimy Ridge by the Canadian Corps. It is a rather understudied battle of the war, even though it had a higher daily casualty rate than the Somme.

Visits

Town Centre

A very handy overnight stop and a pretty, historic, centre. The Grande Place is an ideal place for a good meal; a late night beverage whilst admiring the beautifully lit Town Hall is not to be sniffed at either.

The Vimy Ridge memorial.

Wellington Quarry/Carriére Wellington

A museum and underground series of quarries, used by British forces during their occupation of Arras, that one can visit by means of a very good guided and audio-visual tour. Arras has many such *souterraines* from the medieval period which British and New Zealand tunnellers developed during the war. Visit http://www.explorearras.com/en/visit/remembrance.html, which will also give you useful information on other Arras Great War sites as well.

Arras Memorial

This memorial commemorates 34,795 soldiers of the forces of the United Kingdom, South Africa and New Zealand who have no known grave and who died in the Arras sector of the front. It is located at the Faubourg d'Amiens British CWGC Cemetery. One of the most famous men remembered here is Walter Tull, a black former Tottenham Hotspur player. He was commissioned in 1917, despite British military codes seemingly forbidding this. The memorial to the missing of the Flying Service is also here.

Mur des Fusillés

An approximately fifteen minute walk from the Arras Memorial brings you to this haunting spot, an execution post memorial to the 218 members of the resistance who were executed here by the Nazis during the Second World War. A chill is certain to course down your spine.

Vimy Ridge

One of the author's favourite visits on the Western Front; the beautiful Canadian National Memorial, which stands atop the ridge, overlooking the Douai Plain. This remembers the action by the Canadian Corps who captured this ridge in April 1917, during the Battle of Arras and also stands as a memorial to all Canadian servicemen who died during the war. The names of those killed fighting in France, and who have no known grave, are engraved on the walls of the monument (the equivalent for those in Belgium are on the Menin Gate). It is of immense national importance to Canada; it is argued by some who say, not unreasonably, that Canadian nationhood was truly born here. The whole site is a preserved battlefield park, which bares all the scars of war; part of the park has a restored and preserved trench system which can be freely explored along with a subway (the Grange), which requires a guide. Currently a guided tour of the latter can be taken by a maximum of twenty-five people per time. There are other memorials and two cemeteries contained within this huge site. To book tours, email: vimy.memorial@vac-arc.gc.ca.

Cabaret Rouge CWGC Cemetery

An impressive concentration cemetery containing the remains of 7,656 soldiers. Notably, in 2000, the remains of an unidentified Canadian soldier were removed from Plot 8, Row E, Grave 7 and taken to Ottawa, where they now rest in the Tomb of the Unknown Soldier. A headstone detailing this has replaced the original.

Notre Dame de Lorette French National Memorial and Cemetery

The largest French Military cemetery in the world, sited on land fought over during the three Battles of Artois (1914/15) and containing 39,958 burials, just fewer than 20,000 of whom are unknown. There is a small, but very good, museum and views of the Artois battlefield. French combat operations in the Second World War, Indochina and Algeria are also remembered, with the tombs of unknown warriors from each.

The French cemetery at Douaumont, on the Verdun battlefield, has fewer formal graves, but many thousands of bones collected from the battlefield have been placed in the ossuary there.

Loos

History

On 25 September 1915 the British launched their largest offensive thus far of the war, at Loos. This was an adjunct to another Artois offensive by the French. Overall, little was gained from this assault; ammunition and artillery shortages limited the effectiveness of the artillery bombardment and reserve formations were not deployed well and thus when opportunities for breakthrough did arise, they were not capitalised upon. The Battle of Loos highlighted the problem of communication from front to rear in the First World War. The battle is notable for the first use of gas by the British, which did not work well due to the wind changing direction and engulfing many of the British themselves. British casualties were 43,000 compared to the Germans' 20,000 and the lack of results contributed to the resignation of Sir John French and his replacement by Haig.

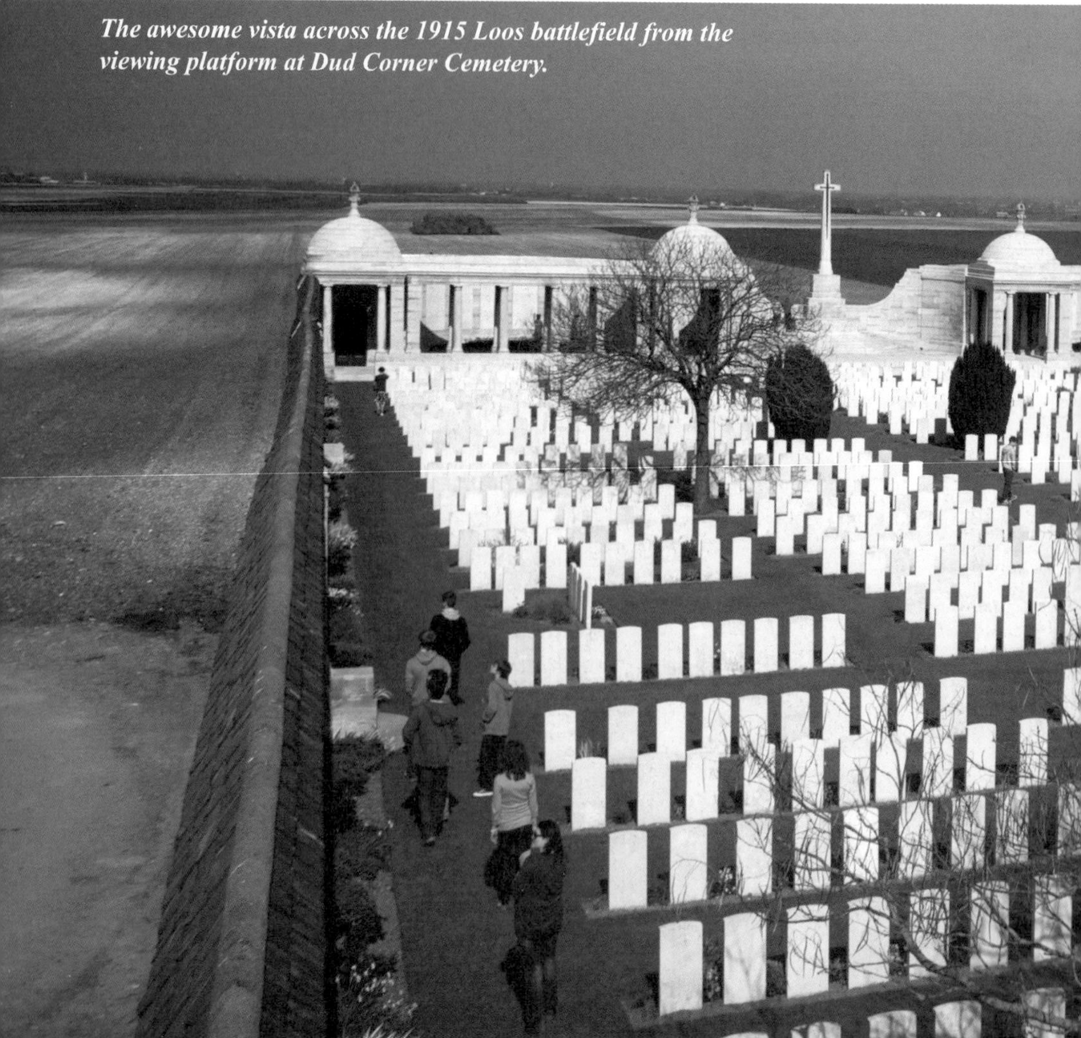

The awesome vista across the 1915 Loos battlefield from the viewing platform at Dud Corner Cemetery.

Visits

Dud Corner CWGC Cemetery and Loos Memorial

There are 1,800 burials in the cemetery and 21,000 names listed on the memorial which commemorates those who fell during the battle but who have no known grave. On the memorial is listed John Kipling, son of Rudyard, who died during the battle [N.B. as of late 2013 it is still there – it is due to be removed at some stage due to the following information]. His father was distraught by the loss and spent his life trying to locate his son's body; he had used his friendship with Lord Roberts, former Commander in Chief of the Army, to secure a place for John in the Irish Guards, despite his very poor eyesight. John was last seen alive stumbling across the battlefield, his face savaged by the effects of artillery. However, in 1992 his body was reportedly identified in St Mary's ADS CWGC Cemetery (see below), but there is doubt over this claim.

There is a wonderful view over the Loos battlefield to be had from the viewing platform that is a feature of the cemetery.

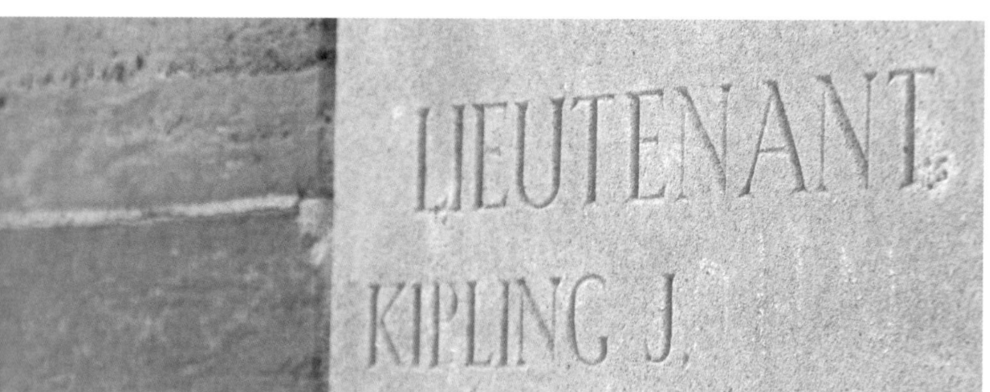

St Mary's ADS CWGC Cemetery

One of the 1,760 burials here is said to be that of Lieutenant John Kipling (VII D 2). Prior to 1992 this was a grave of an unknown Irish Guard lieutenant. However, one researcher suggested that this must actually be Kipling as he was the only man of this regiment and rank missing. Hence, after much examination of the records, the CWGC determined to change the headstone. However, this is disputed, notably by the battlefield historians Tonie and Valmai Holt in their book: *My Boy Jack? The Search for Kipling's Only Son* (Pen & Sword Publishing). Although Kipling had recently been promoted, it was possible that he was still wearing his second lieutenant's badges of rank and, also, this body was found 3.5 miles from where Kipling was last seen.

Neuve Chapelle

History

This was the first deliberately planned large offensive carried out by the British in the war. The Battle of Neuve Chapelle was fought from 10-13 March 1915, with the plan being to break the German lines. The British carried out a huge, but short, bombardment and captured the village of Neuve Chapelle on the first day of the attack. The success seemed to indicate that precision preparation and swift bombardments followed by rapid infantry assault would be the best way to fight this war. Although poor communications, a shortage of shells and a considerable German counter attack brought the allied assault to an end, it had proved to the French that the British could be a valuable fighting force.

Visits

Portuguese Cemetery and Memorial

An interesting visit linked to the Kaiser's Offensive of 1918. A relatively small force of Portuguese soldiers served with the Allied forces, due to colonial rivalry with the Germans and the effects that U-boat warfare was having on Portuguese trade with Britain (Portugal and Britain also have the world's oldest diplomatic alliance, the 1386 Treaty of Windsor – it is still in force today). On 9 April 1918, at the Battle of the Lys, 100,000 German

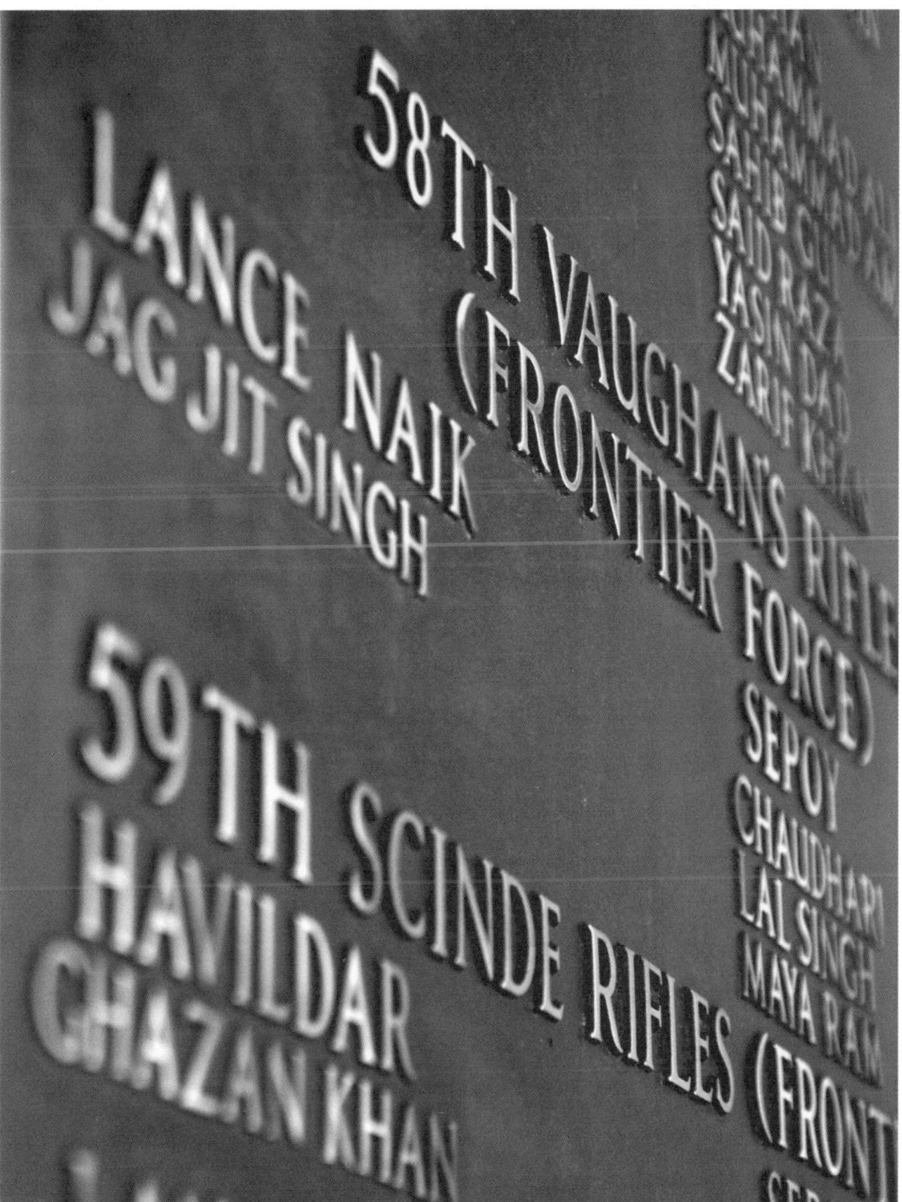

Names on the Neuve Chapelle Indian Memorial.

soldiers descended upon 20,000 exhausted, ill-trained Portuguese who were suffering from poor morale. The result was an inevitable disaster for the Portuguese, with casualties numbering some 7,400.

It was at the Battle of the Lys that Private Aníbal Milhais held up, with his machine gun, the German advance long enough for his comrades to retreat. The Germans

The architecture and designs at the Indian Memorial underline the point that Empire troops were vital to the Allied cause.

eventually simply went around what they thought was an Allied strongpoint and Milhais survived for some days on sweet almonds. He then decided to try to get back to the Allied lines and, to add even more glamour to his tale of heroism, he rescued a Scottish major from drowning in a swamp. The two of them made it back to safety and the thankful Scotsman shared Milhais' story. When he died in 1970, he was regarded as a Portuguese national hero.

Neuve Chapelle Indian Memorial

This is sited near a position known as Port Arthur and is on a part of the line from which men of the Indian Corps left their trench positions on 10 March 1915 to launch their attack. This is a stunning memorial and commemorates the 5,000 men of the Indian Army with no known grave in France. It is very important to note that this is not a memorial to men just from what is now modern day India, but it incorporates all those who were part of the united India of the time such as Bangladesh, Pakistan and Sri Lanka as well as their British officers. It is very interesting for visitors to note the names for ranks and the varied religious symbolism.

Le Touret Memorial

Another wonderful memorial, elaborate and quite beautiful; it lists 13,389 names of those

British soldiers who were killed in this area prior to the Battle of Loos and who have no known grave.

Fromelles

History

An attack, a subsidiary of the battle raging at the Somme, was carried out here on 19-20 July, 1916. The plan was to take advantage of any weakening of the German line at their salient position at Fromelles. That this battle is sometimes referred to as one of the worst twenty four hours in Australian history gives you some idea as to how successful the attack was. The attackers were outnumbered, moving against well established positions, the daylight assault unwise and the whole advance easily overlooked from Aubers Ridge. The Australians lost 5,533 men out of a total loss of 7,000.

Visits

Fromelles Pheasant Wood CWGC Cemetery

Opened in 2010, this is the first new CWGC Cemetery in more than 50 years. The building of this was necessary due to the discovery of mass graves, near the village of Fromelles, which contained the bodies of 250 Australian and British soldiers who died during the battle. Using DNA analysis, work is continuing to identify as many of the men as is possible. A new museum has recently been opened here.

* * *

Further Resources and Web Links

All those books and websites listed below are either directly referenced in this work or were vital research works for the author. I would highly recommend each and every one of them to you:

Guide Books

Coombs R, *Before Endeavours Fade*, After the Battle, Essex, 2006.

Holt T and Holt V, *Major and Mrs Holt's Battlefield Guide to the Somme*, Pen & Sword Military, Barnsley, 2008.

Holt T and Holt V, *Major and Mrs Holt's Battlefield Guide to the Western Front - North*, Pen & Sword Military, Barnsley, 2007.

Holt T and Holt V, *Major and Mrs Holt's Battlefield Guide to the Ypres Salient & Passchendaele*, Pen & Sword Military, Barnsley, 2008.

Horsfall J and Cave N, *Battleground Europe: Mons 1914*, Leo Cooper, Barnsley, 2000.

Rawson A, *Battleground Europe: Loos-Hohenzollern Redoubt*, Leo Cooper, Barnsley, 2003.

Reed P, *Battleground Europe: Walking the Salient*, Leo Cooper, Barnsley, 2008.

Reed P, *Battleground Europe: Walking Arras*, Pen & Sword Military, Barnsley, 2007.

Histories, Biographies and general reference

Black J, *The Great War and the Making of the Modern World*, Continuum, London, 2011.

Brown M, *The Imperial War Museum Book of the Western Front*, Pan Books, London, 2001.

Clark A, *The Donkeys*, Pimlico, London, 1991.

Clark C, *The Sleepwalkers: How Europe Went to War in 1914*, Penguin, London, 2013.

Corrigan G, *Mud, Blood and Poppycock*, Cassell, London, 2004.

Ferguson N, *The Pity of War: 1914-1918*, Penguin, London, 2009.

Fussell P, *The Great War and Modern Memory*, Oxford Paperbacks, Oxford, 2000.

Groom W, *A Storm in Flanders: Triumph and Tragedy on the Western Front*, Cassell, London, 2003.

Hastings M, *Catastrophe: Europe Goes to War 1914*, William Collins, London, 2013.

Holmes R, *Tommy: The British Soldier on the Western Front 1914-1918*, Harper Perennial, London, 2005.

Holt T and Holt V, *My Boy Jack?: the Search for Kipling's Only Son,* Pen & Sword Military, Barnsley, 2007.

Jones N, *The War Walk: A Journey Along the Western Front*, Cassell, London, 2004.

Macdonald L, *Somme*, Penguin Books, London, 1993.

Marix Evans M, *Over The Top: Great Battles of the First World War*, Index, London, 2005.

Masefield J, *The Old Front Line*, Pen & Sword Military, Barnsley, 2006.

Middlebrook M, *The First Day on the Somme*, Allen Lane, London, 1983.

Sheffield G, *Forgotten Victory – The First World War: Myths and Realities*, Headline Book Publishing, London, 2002.

Strachan H, *The First World War*, Free Press, London, 2006.

Van Emden R, *Britain's Last Tommies*, Pen & Sword Military, Barnsley, 2005.

Vaughan E, *Some Desperate Glory: The Diary of a Young Officer, 1917*, Leo Cooper, London, 1982.

Websites

http://firstworldwar.com/ - multimedia history of the war

http://www.battlefields1418.com/ - the brilliant Paul Reed's website

http://www.cwgc.org/ - home of the Commonwealth War Graves Commission

http://www.greatwar.co.uk/ - an outstanding guide to all things First World War and the battlefields themselves

http://www.nationalarchives.gov.uk/pathways/firstworldwar/ - documents and records from the archives

http://www.ww1battlefields.co.uk/index.html - a very good guide to visiting the Western Front

http://www.ww1cemeteries.com/index.htm - another great site dedicated to visiting the Western front

http://fatherdoyle.com/ - Remembering Father William Doyle

We keep the memory alive so that future generations do the same thing.

Acknowledgements

My interest in battlefield touring was fired by two wonderful school trips: one to the Western Front and the other to Normandy. Several years would pass (University!) before I had the chance to visit again. By this stage I had decided to take the leap into the world of teaching and, in a strange twist, I found myself working in the same department that had taught me as a school boy.

Les Shears, Tom Verinder and Paul Franks were outstanding colleagues and they were the ones who "schooled" me in the art of leading group visits to the battlefields. Les, scrupulously musing over his trench maps, a master of the smallest detail and was largely oblivious to the forty students waiting for him to get back on the coach. Franksy, the unlikely hero of the Hull-Zeebrugge ferry dance floor and a man kind enough to politely point out when my spiel was completely incorrect (remember the "quagmire" at Lijssenthoek!?). And Tom, the man who taught me all I know about beer equilibrium and someone I am proud to call my closest friend. I owe them a huge debt, not just for the trips but for shining light on an area of history which has gripped me ever since. We would, of course, be joined on our annual jaunts by the living (just about) legend, Nigel 'why are we here/pass me a Duvel' Owen – a man I cannot begin to explain but one that you are certainly poorer for not knowing. Time moves on, as did I, and the dream team came to an end. To Les and Nige in retirement, Franksy in Saudi Arabia and Tom somewhere in a pub in Wakefield… cheers boys (and sorry if I have stolen most of your spiel for this book)!

In recent years my battlefield buddies have been Adam Hall, Ed Long, Laura Powell, Hannah Biggin, Jonathan Sykes and Jonathan Webb. The Hull-Zeebrugge ferry always knows when Adam has been on board, his desire to get his money's worth on the buffet is legendary; Ed, on the other hand, is just pleased not to have spent his own money. Webby, special thanks too for passing comment on the early drafts of this book – that Cambridge mind is invaluable.

Paul Bennett deserves particular thanks: he has painstakingly trawled through my manuscripts, making correction after correction and never once tiring of that monumental task! Paul is an outstanding battlefield tour leader in his own right – his "run ashore" evenings are particularly good fun and to be whole-heartedly recommended.

A huge thanks to my wife, Rachel, who became the official photographer for this book. Almost all the photos were taken either by her or by Mike McKinstry, a very talented student and photographer who came on a trip some years ago and took beautiful pictures which I have always intended to use in some way; finally I have a reason! I also thank my father, mother in law and daughter (19 months old at the time!) for putting up with being dragged around the Western Front, with Rachel and me, in the summer of 2013. So to Graham, Denise and Claudia – you were marvellous company!

The wonderful people at Pen & Sword deserve so much praise. Henry Wilson is the man who took a naive teacher with a vague idea for a book and made it into a reality; he took a risk and I am delighted that he did. Matt Jones has steered me in the right direction on numerous occasions and Jon Wilkinson designed a quite brilliant cover. Finally, you have Nigel Cave to thank for this book being credible and actually readable. Nigel, battlefield expert/author/editor of the *Battleground Europe* series and all round good egg, is the best copy editor/fact checker/suggestion-maker that I could have hoped for. Without him this book would simply not have been good enough; I owe him a huge debt. In fact, I do not think that I dare write anything in future unless he casts an eye over it first!

Finally, thank you to every student who ever came on one of my tours – you are the reason that I keep doing this and, more importantly, keep loving doing it.

GJH, March 2014

* * *

Permissions

I am hugely grateful for the permission granted to publish extracts from the following sources:

A Storm in Flanders by Winston Groom (Orion Publishing).

The Old Front Line by John Masefield (The Society of Authors and Pen & Sword Publishing).

"The Sentry" by Wilfred Owen in Wilfred Owen: The War Poems (Chatto & Windus, 1994); Editor: Jon Stallworthy.

Extracts from the diary of Father William Doyle; http://fatherdoyle.com/.

Pen & Sword Publishing for all of their help in securing permissions from titles in their catalogue.

Wherever a work is quoted or used in the text I have made every effort to secure permission from the relevant source. I will happily update and amend, where required, in any future edition.

Index